sewing kids' stuff

Fun Things for Kids to Wear and Share

By The Editors Of

SEW NEWS

PJS Publications Inc. Peoria, Illinois

PJS Publications Inc., News Plaza, Box 1790, Peoria, IL 61656

ISBN
0-9621148-3-9

Copyright© 1991

Library of Congress
No. 91-90458

sewing kids' stuff

Cindy Kacynski: Book Editor

Ann Nunemacher & Lucy Blunier: Illustrators

Jan Ebling: Photography Stylist

Darrel K. Freisinger, Color Classics Portrait Studio: Photographer

Pudik Art Studios Inc.: Book Production

Staff at PJS Publications Inc.:

SEW NEWS Editorial

Linda Turner Griepentrog: Editor

Susan Voigt-Reising: Managing Editor

Annette Gentry Bailey: Assistant Editor

Circulation/Marketing

Cherine Sank: Promotion Manager

Julie Luchtefeld: Fulfillment Assistant

Publisher

Jerry R. Constantino: President

Del Rusher: Vice President/Creative Woman's Group Publisher

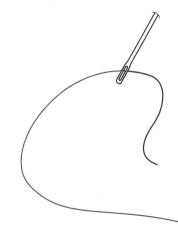

By The Editors Of

SEW NEWS
THE FASHION MAGAZINE FOR PEOPLE WHO SEW

ACKNOWLEDGEMENTS

SEW NEWS has dedicated many pages to sewing for kids throughout the years, but the recent "baby boom" has peaked our interest in this area of sewing even more. Thus, the introduction of "Kidding Around," a quarterly column devoted to sewing for the little ones in our lives. Based on the response we've received, we are addressing a topic near and dear to many a reader's heart. Fashion-sewers want to sew for children for both practical and creative reasons.

This inspired us to produce a book on the subject. SEWING KIDS' STUFF is a compilation of child-oriented projects (accessories, costumes, apparel, decor items and more), a few of which were previously published in SEW NEWS and many new designs.

SEWING KIDS' STUFF has drawn from the creative wisdom of not only the SEW NEWS editorial staff, but a host of contributing writers as well: Evelyn Brannon, Alma Burge, Beth Ann Cecchettini, Judy Darden, Barbara Dimmitt, Laurie Eastwood, Sue Green-Baker, Sue Greer, Barb Griffin, Frances Grimble, Grace Johnson, Ellen Kendrick, Cindy King, Katie Kingston, Janet Klaer, Sandra Kritschgau, Jane Meyer, Ann Price, Nancy Nix Rice, Anne Marie Soto, Pat Watson and Barbara Weiland. We appreciate the creative hand you offered in producing this book.

We would also like to give special thanks to our talented and conscientious dressmaker, Sue Barnabee, for her creativity and tenacity in sewing many of the projects shown throughout SEWING KIDS' STUFF.

And thanks to the dedicated SEW NEWS readers who have inspired us by their continual feedback and encouragement to produce SEWING KIDS' STUFF.

By The Editors Of

TABLE OF CONTENTS

* Full-size pattern offer at end of article

HELPFUL EXTRAS

To assist you in creating the projects listed in the Table of Contents and featured in color photos on pages 7 through 22 and to offer you some useful sewing tips to complement your hobby, we have compiled several "Helpful Extras" and sprinkled them throughout SEWING KIDS' STUFF. Use these tips and techniques as handy references for all your sewing-for-children endeavors to achieve the quickest, easiest, most professional results.

sewing
kids'
stuff

NOTABLE TOTABLES

A sprightly quilted lunch bag/placemat combination packs a pretty snack for noontime nibbling at school, day camp or in your own backyard.

"Snack-Packer"
(refer to instructions on page 33)

Toting toys or togs is fun stuff for the child sporting his or her own drawstring toy sack (right)— embellished to the child's delight—or quilted soft luggage (left) sewn in festive primaries.

"Kid-Little Luggage"
(refer to instructions on page 28)

"Toy Tote-Along"
(refer to instructions on page 36)

SEW-SPOOKY COSTUMING

Jack-O-Lantern   Drum Major   Muscle Man   Skeleton   Ballerina

"Terror-ific!"
(refer to instructions on page 41)

Kids will love choosing an "assumed identity" for an evening of Halloween magic or another dress-up event—and you'll adore sewing one of these simple creations for a speedy (and affordable!) costume for your favorite little goblin.

Devil   **Witch**

Court Jester   **Bunny**

"Halloween In A Hurry"
(refer to instructions on page 43)

Sweatsuits form the base for the costumes in *"Halloween In A Hurry"* and *"Devil Duty,"* but the results are anything but impetuous—the attention to detail will capture the hearts of kids young and old. And your little *"good witch"* will put magic into the evening in her authentic, but jovial, hat and cape (*"Bewitching Capers"*).

"Devil Duty"
(refer to instructions on page 47)

"Bewitching Capers"
(refer to instructions on page 49)

KIDS'-ROOM CAPERS

A child's bedroom is his or her haven, and you can help make the room extra special with accessories both fun and functional. A hairbow caddy (right) to house headbands, ribbons, scrunchies, etc., makes a fun wall accent, while a quilt embellished with your child's own handprints (below) makes a festive wall hanging and a precious keepsake. Preparing for a new arrival? Sew an extra special designer nursery (far right)—in a matter of hours!

"Hairport Hanger"

(refer to instructions on page 63)

"Hand-Printed Keepsake"

(refer to instructions on page 60)

"Babes In Nurseryland"

(refer to instructions on page 55)

TOYS/TIME FOR FUN

Baby will love appliquéd soft blocks (below) for learning letters, colors and shapes, while bath time promises nothing but fun with an appliquéd bear bath mitt and towel duo (right).

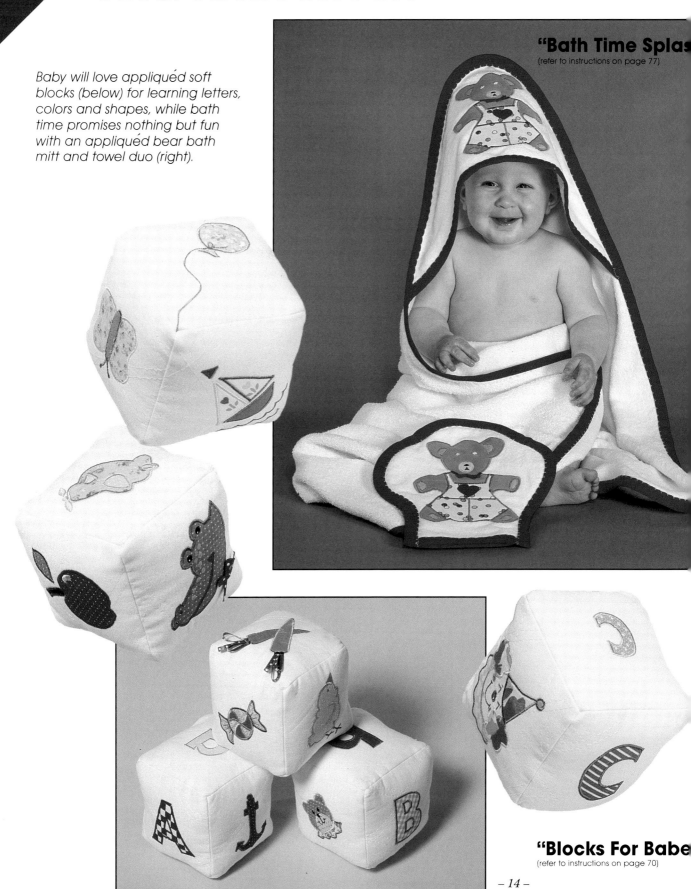

"Bath Time Splas
(refer to instructions on page 77)

"Blocks For Babe
(refer to instructions on page 70)

"Tiny Town"
(refer to instructions on page 68)

...ds will get a kick out of
...king this playtime town on
...e road, its unique con-
...uction allowing him or her
...simply pull the drawstring
...convert it into a toy tote.

An Ultrasuede® vest and chaps duo puts your
little wrangler (boys and girls alike!) on the (play)
range in style for dress-up fun or clever costuming.

"Cowboy Kudos"
(refer to instructions on page 80)

LITTLE TOUCHES

A splashy book bag (right), replete with drawstring/flap closure and accessory pouch, packs a punch (and a lunch, notebooks, pencils and other school-time essentials!) for back-to-school fun. Little ones will squeal with delight when donning one of these sprightly bibs (below) embellished to suit any occasion.

"Bitty Book Bag"

(refer to instructions on page 99)

Mr. Irresistible Bib

Gerry Giraffe Bib

Party Perfect

"Drool-Cool Bibs"

(refer to instructions on page 89)

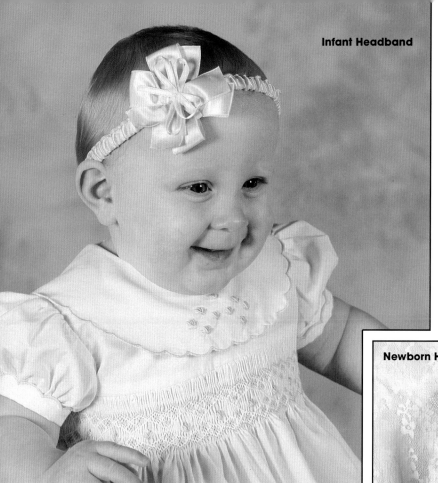

Infant Headband

"Banded Beauty"
(refer to instructions on page 97)

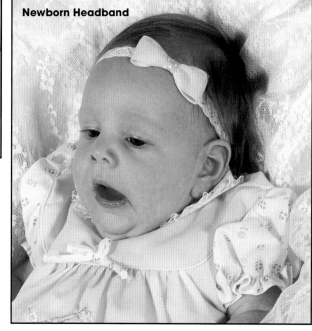

Newborn Headband

Tiny headbands for newborns and infants (above and right) say "It's a girl!" in an oh-so-feminine fashion, while pouf socks (below) are simple extras that can be coordinated with any outfit for a creative, lively look.

"Fancy Feet"
(refer to instructions on page 87)

KIDS CAN SEW, TOO!

Get children into the spirit of sewing with simple-to-create projects, such as this shop apron for the little carpenter (right), featuring a simple drawstring casing for easy-fit and compartments for all his necessary extras. Or, consider a montage of easy-sew gifts (below) to encourage creativity as well as generosity.

"Tool Cool"
(refer to instructions on page 117)

"Sew Gifted"
(refer to instructions on page 109)

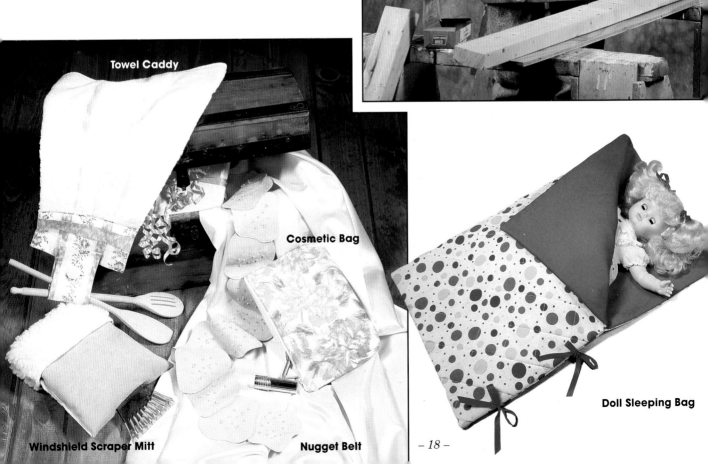

Towel Caddy

Cosmetic Bag

Windshield Scraper Mitt

Nugget Belt

Doll Sleeping Bag

"Serger Kids"
(refer to instructions on page 121)

Introduce your little one to the magical world of sergers. This simple sweatshirt will be a snap to create— even for the novice. And she'll love embellishing it with bows, buttons, baubles . . .

ART TO WEAR

Wearable art will wow your little one with its bevy of applications in children's clothing and accessories! Use appliqué, color-blocking, button-art and other surface embellishments independently or collectively in unique combinations to make artistic, whimsical statements in both fashion and fun.

"Bow-Dacious"
(refer to instructions on page 135)

"Bloomin' Bloomers"
(refer to instructions on page 131)

Cherries Jubilee Panties

Sweet Hearts Panties

Floral Fantasy Panties

"Cute As A Button"
(refer to instructions on page 142)

Sprightly Suspenders

Multi-Motif Sneakers

"Catching Some Gs"
(refer to instructions on page 127)

"Workout Wow!"
(refer to instructions on page 138)

SEW, YOU'RE A MOM!

"Baby Frame-Up

(refer to instructions on page 146)

"Baby Cuddle-Up" (blanket)

(refer to instructions on page 159)

"Baptismal Bliss" (gown)

(refer to instructions on page 153)

Loving stitches set a caring foundation for baby's arrival as new moms (or grandmothe or aunts!) sew for the little cherub such keepsakes as fabric frames (above), a receiving blanket and christening gown (left and a Christmas stocking (below).

"Baby's First Christmas"

(refer to instructions on page 150)

INTRODUCTION

Sewing for kids might bring to mind images of fun or frustration, creativity or challenge, bonding or conflict. And undertaking such a task could feasibly yield any of the above. The process of matching your sewing skill level and opinions about style, color, etc., with your child's own ideas about what he or she will use or wear can test even the closest parent/child relationship. It more likely will prove to enhance a relationship when the finished project meets or exceeds your expectations—and your child's.

The secret to this success: working together and respecting one another's opinions, likes and dislikes. SEWING KIDS' STUFF encourages this throughout its 11 chapters, trying to make the most of kids' untapped creativity, moms' (or aunts' or grandmas' or even dads'!) sewing skills.

This is a creative project book that details fun sewing ideas for adults and children, with some projects simple enough for kids to sew themselves. It takes a light-hearted approach to creating simple-to-sew designs with elaborate results. These designs rival ready-mades in terms of style, surpass ready-mades in quality of construction and creative application. You and your child are the ultimate "designers" of these projects, we simply guide you along.

Whether you're sewing for a newborn or a 10-year-old, a girl or a boy, a choosy pre-teen or a go-with-the-flow preschooler, you'll find inspiration on the following pages. We've tried to give you a sampling of many different types of projects—from toys to togs—so you can pick and choose what meets your current needs. Feel free to embellish upon our ideas to make the designs your very own, choosing different fabrics or notions to execute the looks. And be sure to keep in mind that the more involved your child is in each project (from selecting fabrics to actual sewing), the more likely he or she will be to use and take pride in the finished piece. This will also foster creativity and a stronger bond between you and your child.

The following articles include illustrated, step-by-step instructions, many with graphed patterns, and you'll notice they indulge the same style you've become accustomed to when reading SEW NEWS. Some stories focus more on inspiration, but most detail every step necessary to achieve the results seen in the color photographs on pages 7 through 22. As an additional benefit, we offer you the opportunity to acquire full-sized patterns for some projects at the conclusion of certain articles.

Super-simple Halloween costumes, a nursery decorating plan, kids' luggage, appliquéd soft blocks, Ultrasuede® chaps and vest, a tool apron, a color-blocked leotard and a christening gown are just a sampling of the more than 50 projects featured in SEWING KIDS' STUFF. And the book concludes with chapters dedicated solely to making a plan for sewing apparel for your children—complete with ideas for accurate measuring, adding growth features and alterations—and sewing clothing kids *will* wear.

We hope you enjoy SEWING KIDS' STUFF and it inspires creativity in you and your child. But, most importantly, we hope you enjoy sewing for your child. It could be a lesson in patience, but more likely it will be a labor of love. ❏

NOTABLE TOTABLES

Kids are mobile little creatures who love to "take their show on the road," so to speak. Packing up their own small-but-mighty belongings—toys, togs and treats—is a natural for them, affording added security, and often something to do, for short jaunts or long journeys away from home. Totes have become ever-present on the fashion scene, too, and children can't help but notice all the nifty ways they can tow their treasures to and from school, Grandma's, the babysitter's, vacation desti-nations or just out to play.

Our most notable tota-bles (refer to the photos on pages 8 and 9) will meet a child's every need and will be as simple or detailed a sewing activity as mom would like to undertake. These are projects that can involve the kids, too, in terms of color, fabric and embellishment selections. In fact, "Toy Tote-Along" is a wonderfully simple first project for even the most inexperienced child sewer to try—with your close supervision, of course. *Note:* See "Keeping Children In Stitches" on page 106 for tips on teach-ing children to sew.

Use your creativity when sewing these carry-alls—don't limit yourself just to the uses shown. For exam-ple, the duffle in "Kid's Little Luggage" would be a great sports bag for little athletes to stow their soc-cer shirt and shoes or dancers to pack away their tap shoes and tutus. The "Snack Packer" goes to school with older kids or is something special for the younger set to take to the sitter's or day care center for a mid-morning snack or mid-day lunch. And the

"Toy Tote-Along"...the possibilities are endless; it can be used for everything from carrying library and school books to toting all the necessities for slumber parties and weekend overnights—not to mention the obvious: toting those prized toys.

These simple-to-make totes are fun sewing ventures for you and your child, so get inspired—if you sew 'em, they'll tote 'em! ❏

kid-little luggage

Kids on the go will love this traveling duo, just the right size for packing all their important gear. Make the zip-up garment bag and duffle in primary colors to appeal to any little jet-setter, whether he's off to camp, Grandma's or a trek around the world. You'll love the easy sewing and easy care of these wash-and-wear pieces, not to mention their minimal cost compared to ready-mades.

GARMENT BAG

MATERIALS

• ⅞ yard of 45"-wide double-faced quilted juvenile print. *Note:* If you would prefer to quilt your own fabric, see "Quilt It Quick" on page 38 for instructions.

• ⅝ yard of sturdy cotton or cotton blend fabric to contrast or coordinate with the quilted fabric

• 24"-long separating sport zipper with oversized plastic teeth in a color to contrast with the quilted fabric

• Two 2½-yard packages of ⅛"-diameter piping in the same color as the zipper

• Two 4¼"x10" strips of mediumweight fusible interfacing

• 7" of ⅛"-wide grosgrain ribbon in a color to contrast with the zipper

• Pattern tracing cloth

CUTTING

■ Enlarge the pattern pieces in Figure 1 and cut two bag fronts and one bag back from the quilted fabric.

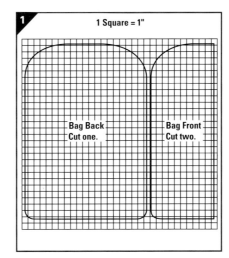

1 Square = 1"

Bag Back Cut one.

Bag Front Cut two.

■ From the coordinating fabric, cut four 4"x44" strips for the bag bands, two 4¼"x10" strips for the handles and one 2"x5½" strip and one 2"x4¼" strip for the zipper trims.

CONSTRUCTION

Note: Use ⅝" seam allowances throughout unless otherwise indicated.

■ Serge- or zigzag-finish all edges of the bag front and back pieces.

■ Press under a seam allowance at the long straight edge of each bag front. Position the bag front pieces right sides up with the folded edges matching.

■ Position the zipper stop 1¾" above the lower edge of the bag fronts, with the pressed-under edges as close to the zipper teeth as possible. Using a zipper foot, stitch as close to the fold as possible, securing the zipper long edges (Figure 2).

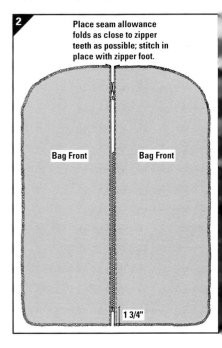

Place seam allowance folds as close to zipper teeth as possible; stitch in place with zipper foot.

Bag Front

Bag Front

1 3/4"

■ Fold the 2"x5½" zipper trim strip in half crosswise, right sides together, and stitch each long raw edge in a ¼" seam (Figure 3).

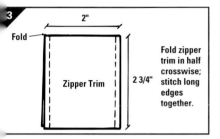

3

Fold

2"

Zipper Trim

2 3/4"

Fold zipper trim in half crosswise; stitch long edges together.

■ Turn the trim right side out and press, then center it over the zipper lower edge, with the folded end covering the last 1" of the zipper teeth. Edgestitch in place up to, but not across, the zipper teeth (Figure 4). Repeat with the remaining zipper trim strip, positioning the folded end just above the zipper pull; edgestitch in place along the three finished edges (Figure 5).

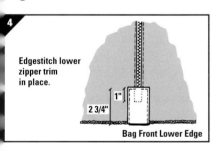

4

Edgestitch lower zipper trim in place.

2 3/4"

1"

Bag Front Lower Edge

■ Wrong sides together, machine baste two band strips together along the 44" edges. Repeat with the remaining band strips. Serge- or zigzag-finish all of the band edges.

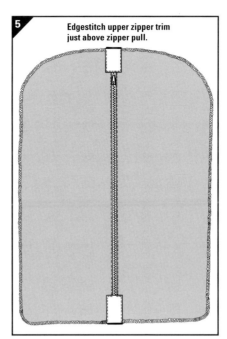

5 Edgestitch upper zipper trim just above zipper pull.

■ Right sides together, stitch the two bands together end to end in a ¼" seam to create one long band; press the seam open.

■ Narrowly hem the remaining short ends of the band by pressing under ¼", then another ⅜", and edgestitching in place.

■ Using a basting stitch and contrasting-color thread in the bobbin, apply piping to both long edges of the band along the seamline, angling the ends into the seam allowance at the finished ends (Figure 6).

■ Fold the bag back in half lengthwise and snip-mark the center fold at the upper and lower edges (Figure 7).

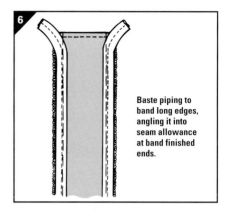

6

Baste piping to band long edges, angling it into seam allowance at band finished ends.

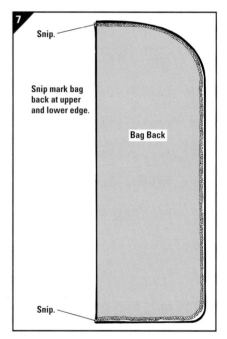

7

Snip.

Snip mark bag back at upper and lower edge.

Bag Back

Snip.

■ Fuse one interfacing strip to one handle strip wrong side, then fold the handle strip in half lengthwise, right sides together, and stitch the long raw edges together. Trim the seams to ¼", turn the handle right side out and press; edgestitch.

Repeat with the remaining handle and interfacing strips.

■ Right sides together and raw edges matching, center one end of one finished handle on the bag back upper edge, one end of the other handle on the lower edge, over the center snip marks; machine baste in place (Figure 8).

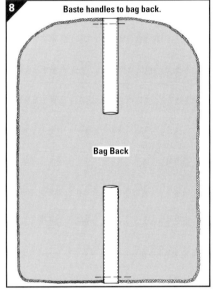
Baste handles to bag back.

Bag Back

■ Right sides together, pin the band to the bag back, matching the band seam to the bag back's lower edge snip-mark. *Note:* The bands' upper ends should butt together at the bag's upper edge snip-mark and will remain unattached for hanger hook placement. Stitch in place from the band side, following the contrasting-color piping basting line and using a zipper foot to get as close as possible to the piping (Figure 9).

■ Unzip the zipper in the bag front.

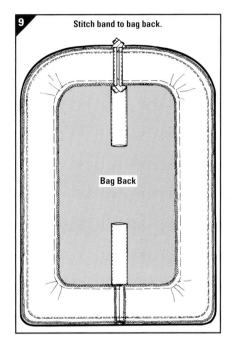
Stitch band to bag back.

Bag Back

■ Right sides together, pin the bag front to the remaining band edge. Stitch, centering and catching the remaining end of each handle in the seam (Figure 10).

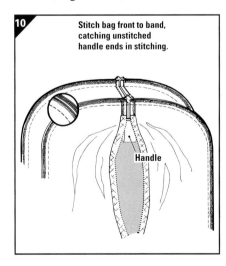
Stitch bag front to band, catching unstitched handle ends in stitching.

Handle

■ Turn the bag right side out and loop the ribbon through the zipper pull hole to help tiny fingers maneuver the closure (Figure 11).

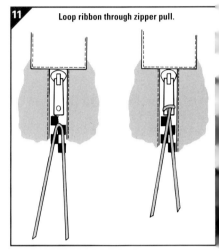
Loop ribbon through zipper pull.

DUFFLE BAG

MATERIALS

• ½ yard of 45"-wide quilted juvenile print. *Note:* If you would prefer to quilt your own fabric, see "Quilt It Quick" on page 38 for instructions.

• ½ yard of sturdy cotton or cotton blend fabric to coordinate or contrast with the quilted fabric

• One 9"-long zipper

• One 2½-yard package of ⅛"-diameter piping in the same color as the zipper

• 7" of ⅛"-wide grosgrain ribbon in a color to contrast with the zipper

• Two 8¼" squares of mediumweight fusible interfacing (optional)

CUTTING

■ Cut two 10¾"x15¼" rectangles from the quilted fabric for the bag.

■ From the coordinating fabric, cut two 8¼" squares for the bag ends and two 4¼"x42" strips for the handles.

CONSTRUCTION

Note: Use ⅝" seam allowances throughout unless otherwise indicated.

■ Serge- or zigzag-finish all edges of the bag and bag end pieces.

■ Stitch the bag rectangles together along one 10¾" end. Press the seam open and topstitch the seam allowances in place ¼" from the seam (Figure 12).

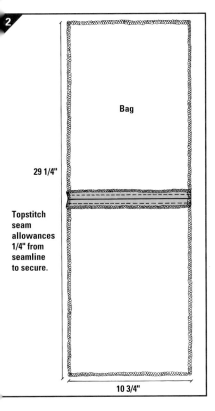

29 1/4"

Topstitch seam allowances 1/4" from seamline to secure.

Bag

10 3/4"

■ Using a basting stitch and contrasting-color thread in the bobbin, apply piping to both long edges of the bag at the seamline, angling the piping ends into the seam allowance at the bag short edges (Figure 13).

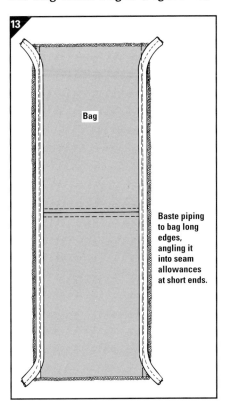

Bag

Baste piping to bag long edges, angling it into seam allowances at short ends.

■ Stitch the handle strips right sides together along one short end; trim the seam and press it open.

■ Fold the handle in half lengthwise, right sides together, and stitch along all three raw edges, leaving an opening for turning. Trim the seam, turn the handle right side out and press, turning in the edges of the opening. Edgestitch around the completed handle.

■ Place the bag right side up on a flat surface. Pin the handle to the bag right side, with one handle edge next to the piping, beginning and ending at the bag seam (Figure 14).

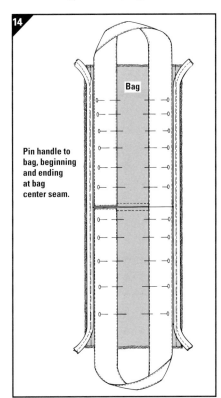

Bag

Pin handle to bag, beginning and ending at bag center seam.

Bag

Beginning at the bag seam, edgestitch the handle in place in four individual 10½"-long rectangles as shown in Figure 15, page 32.

■ Fold the bag in half, wrong sides together, so the short ends meet. With the handles tucked inside and out of the stitching path, stitch these ends together, basting the center 9" for the zipper opening (Figure 16, page 32). Press the seam open.

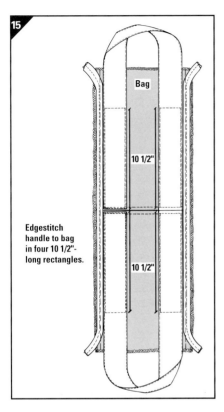

15

Bag

10 1/2"

10 1/2"

Edgestitch handle to bag in four 10 1/2"-long rectangles.

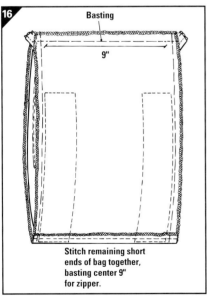

16

Basting

9"

Stitch remaining short ends of bag together, basting center 9" for zipper.

■ Insert the zipper, using a centered application. From the right side, stitch across both zipper ends (Figure 17). Remove the basting in the zipper area.

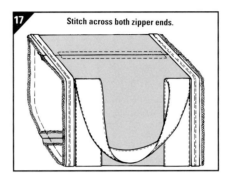

17 Stitch across both zipper ends.

■ Unzip the zipper and turn the bag wrong side out.

■ Stabilize the bag ends by fusing an interfacing square to the wrong side of each or by quilting the fabric (see "Quilt It Quick" on page 38 for instructions).

■ Fold each bag end in half and snip mark the fold at both edges.

■ Right sides together, pin one bag end to the bag, matching one snip mark to the bag bottom seamline, the other to the zipper seamline and clipping the bag seam to the piping stitching line as necessary to fit around the bag end corners (Figure 18). Beginning at the bag bottom seamline, stitch the bag to the bag end from the bag side, following the contrasting-color piping basting line and using a zipper foot to get as close as possible to the piping.

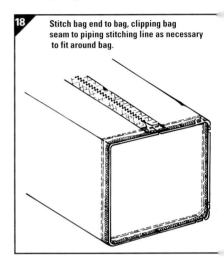

18 Stitch bag end to bag, clipping bag seam to piping stitching line as necessary to fit around bag.

Repeat with the remaining bag end.

■ Turn the bag right side out and loop the ribbon through the zipper pull hole (refer back to Figure 11).

snack-packer

This quilted lunch-box has a special surprise for your little noontime nibbler. The front panel detaches to become a novel placemat for the desk, and two front panels conveniently store nifty napkins and plastic utensils to match.

Choose your child's favorite colors and sew this lunchtime treat into a favorite tote-along for school days—and play days, too!

MATERIALS

- ⅝ yard of 45"-wide, reversible quilted fabric
- 7 yards of extra-wide, double-fold bias tape to contrast or coordinate with fabric
- 2 yards of 1"-wide nylon webbing to contrast or coordinate with fabric
- 8" of ½"-wide hook-and-loop tape, such as Velcro®
- Matching thread
- Air- or water-soluble marker

CONSTRUCTION

■ Enlarge the patterns in Figure 1. From the quilted fabric, cut one lunchbox body, two lunchbox sides, one placemat, one 9" square for the lunchbox front, one 5½"x9" rectangle for the lunchbox bottom and one 4½"x9" rectangle for the lunchbox pocket.

■ Encase one edge of the lunchbox front in bias tape to create the upper edge; repeat along one 9" edge of the lunchbox pocket.

■ Cut two 2"-long pieces of hook-and-loop tape, then position one hook section on the lunchbox pocket right side at each lower edge corner ¾" from the side and lower edges; edgestitch in place (Figure 2).

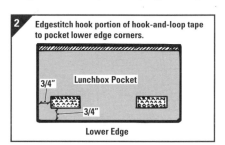

2 Edgestitch hook portion of hook-and-loop tape to pocket lower edge corners.

Lunchbox Pocket

3/4"

3/4"

Lower Edge

■ Baste the pocket to the lunchbox front, with the pocket wrong side against the front right side. Create pocket compartments by topstitching from the pocket lower edge to the upper edge 3" from each side edge, creating three 3"-wide pocket sections (Figure 3, page 34).

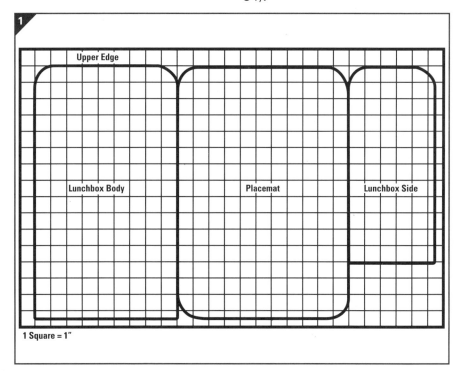

1

Upper Edge

Lunchbox Body

Placemat

Lunchbox Side

1 Square = 1"

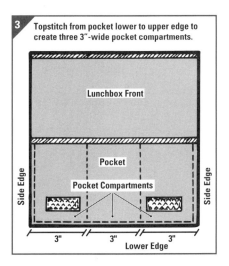

3 Topstitch from pocket lower to upper edge to create three 3"-wide pocket compartments.

Lunchbox Front

Pocket

Pocket Compartments

Side Edge

Side Edge

3" 3" 3"

Lower Edge

■ Mark each lunchbox body side edge 7" from the upper edge, then reinforce this area by stitching along the ½" seamline for 1"; clip the seam allowance to the reinforcement stitching (Figure 4). Apply seam sealant to each clip and allow it to dry.

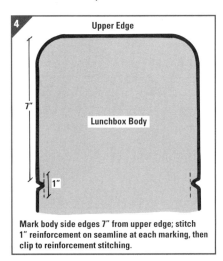

4 Upper Edge

7"

Lunchbox Body

1"

Mark body side edges 7" from upper edge; stitch 1" reinforcement on seamline at each marking, then clip to reinforcement stitching.

■ Use bias tape to encase the lunchbox body upper and side edges between the clips, folding the bias tape under at each clip to completely enclose the

cut edges as you finish stitching.

■ Cut the remaining hook-and-loop tape into two 2"-long pieces and edgestitch the hook portions to the lunchbox body wrong side, positioning one at each upper edge corner, ¾" from the side and upper edges (Figure 5).

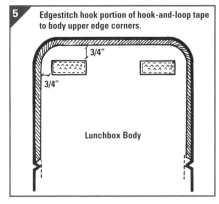

5 Edgestitch hook portion of hook-and-loop tape to body upper edge corners.

¾"

¾"

Lunchbox Body

■ Encase the placemat raw edges in bias tape, turning under the bias tape cut end to finish.

■ Edgestitch one loop piece of hook-and-loop tape to each lower edge corner on the placemat right side, positioning each ¾" from the side and lower edges; edgestitch the remaining two loop pieces to the upper edge corners on the placemat right side, positioning each 4" from the side edges and 3" from the upper edge (Figure 6).

■ Wrong sides together, stitch the lunchbox front/pocket to the lunchbox bottom along the lower edges in a ½" seam; wrong sides together, stitch

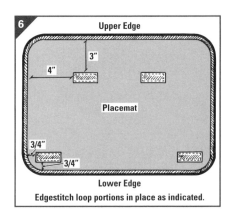

6 Upper Edge

3"

4"

Placemat

¾"

¾"

Lower Edge

Edgestitch loop portions in place as indicated.

the lunchbox bottom upper edge to the lunchbox body lower edge in a ½" seam. Encase each seam allowance in bias tape and press the bound seams up.

■ Closely zigzag the webbing (strap) raw ends or treat them with seam sealant to prevent fraying.

■ Lay the stitched-together lunchbox right side up. Pin the strap in place 1¼" from the side edges as shown, beginning and ending 2½" up from the lunchbox bottom lower edge and abutting the strap ends (Figure 7, page 35).

■ Edgestitch the strap in place, beginning at the lunchbox bottom lower edge and stitching along the lunchbox bottom and body only, stopping the stitching 7" from the body upper edge at each side and at the lunchbox bottom lower edge at each side; reinforce the four ending points by stitching a box with an X through it (Figure 8, page 35).

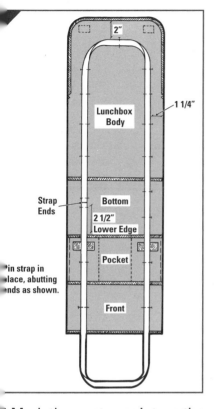

Figure with labels: 2", Lunchbox Body, 1 1/4", Strap Ends, Bottom, 2 1/2", Lower Edge, Pocket, Front. Pin strap in place, abutting ends as shown.

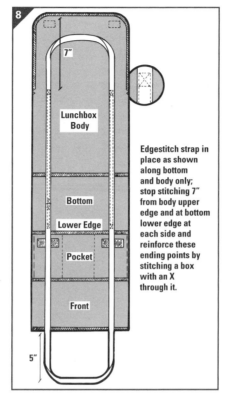

8

7", Lunchbox Body, Bottom, Lower Edge, Pocket, Front, 5"

Edgestitch strap in place as shown along bottom and body only; stop stitching 7" from body upper edge and at bottom lower edge at each side and reinforce these ending points by stitching a box with an X through it.

mat short ends to the wrong side, match the placemat's hook-and-loop tape loop pieces to the hook pieces on the lunchbox front/pocket and fold the placemat upper edge to the lunchbox inside; fold the lunchbox body upper edge to the lunchbox front and match the body's hook-and-loop tape hook pieces onto the loop pieces on the placemat (Figure 9).

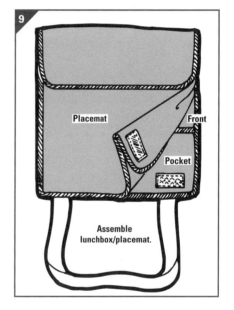

9

Placemat, Front, Pocket

Assemble lunchbox/placemat.

■ Mark the center point on the straight short end of each lunchbox side piece; also mark the center point on the lunchbox bottom side raw edges.

■ Wrong sides together and matching center markings, stitch the sides to the lunchbox front/pocket, bottom and body, leaving the body free above the clips. Encase the raw edges in bias tape.

■ To assemble the lunchbox and placemat: Fold the place-

❏

toy tote-along

Vacation time can be both exciting and confusing, as adults get organized and children sometimes get lost in the shuffle. Spend a few minutes prior to your departure to make this simple tote bag, and your youngster can have his own personal space for packing prized and private treasures. Allow the child to embellish the tote for a truly personalized effort.

DESIGN IDEAS

Most children will enjoy using their rampant imagination to design the tote, however, the child's age, dexterity and artistic abilities should be considered when choosing the design medium. These tips will help.

■ Assist the child in choosing the tote theme. Some ideas:

• A logo to represent the vacation destination, such as the sun for a trip to the ocean or snowflakes for a skiing vacation

• The child's initials embellished into caricatures (Figure 1)

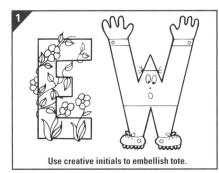

Use creative initials to embellish tote.

• Simple animal motifs

• A stylized version of a tracing of the child's hands or feet (Figure 2)

Enliven a child's footprint for an embellishment option.

■ Use fabric paints, special crayons or markers, available in a wide color range, so your child can draw directly onto the tote fabric; you can later heat-set the masterpiece to make it colorfast.

■ Consider iron-on transfer and letters as other embellishment alternatives.

■ Encourage the child to seek design inspiration from a coloring book, then you can appliqué the motif in place by hand, machine or fusing.

■ Encourage the child to use lots of color—he will treasure the tote longer if he has created some design excitement.

■ If you are teaching the child to sew, suggest the addition of a tiny pocket to hold a prize, coin or special drawing crayon, then let him sew the pocket in place, even if you later need to reinforce it "in the dark of the night."

■ Add the child's name, address and phone number to the tote inside, just in case the child, the tote or both become separated from each other (or you).

MATERIALS

• ½ yard of sturdy fabric, such as denim or canvas. Note: Choose a light-colored, washable fabric that will showcase your child's artwork.

• 1¼ yards of ½"-diameter heavy cording

• Air- or water-soluble marker

• Matching thread

CONSTRUCTION

■ Cut the fabric into two 8"x20" rectangles for the tote front and back.

■ Using an air or water-soluble marker, draw border lines on each fabric rectangle right side ⅝" from the side and lower raw edges and 1¼" from the upper raw edge (Figure 3). These lines will give the child perimeters in which to work.

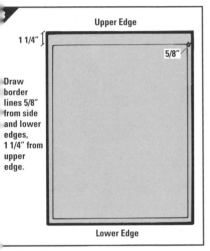

1 1/4"

Upper Edge

5/8"

Draw border lines 5/8" from side and lower edges, 1 1/4" from upper edge.

Lower Edge

■ Anchor the fabric so it will not move around during the "creative process" by stretching and pinning it right side up over a magazine, then taping the edges to a plastic-covered tabletop.

■ Allow the child to embellish the bag front and back.

■ Raw edges matching, pin the tote front and back right sides together; stitch in a ⅝" seam along the side and lower edges only, then stitch again ⅛" from the first stitching inside the seam allowance for reinforcement (Figure 4).

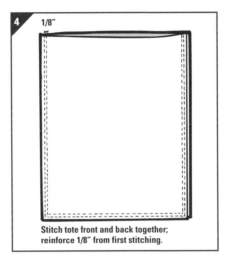

4 1/8"

Stitch tote front and back together; reinforce 1/8" from first stitching.

■ Trim the tote's lower edge corners, then press the side and lower edge seams open (Figure 5).

5

Trim corners, then press seams open.

■ Press under the tote upper edge ¼", then 1"; stitch the upper edge hem close to the first fold, leaving a 2" opening for inserting the cording (Figure 6).

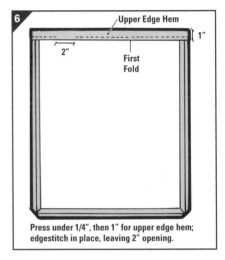

6

Upper Edge Hem

1"

2"

First Fold

Press under 1/4", then 1" for upper edge hem; edgestitch in place, leaving 2" opening.

■ Thread the cording through the casing using a large safety pin or bodkin. Tie the ends into a strong knot. Apply seam sealant to the cording ends to prevent raveling. ❏

— KID-BITS —

Children's clothing of the Victorian era was often made of upholstery-type fabrics and trims.

If you would like to quilt your own print fabric, simply purchase a little extra fabric for your project and the same amount of a single-faced channel-quilted, solid-color fabric.

If you're unable to find channel-quilted fabric:

Purchase equal amounts of a solid-colored fabric and polyester batting; place the fabric right side up on the batting, with raw edges even, and baste together around the outer edges; use an air-soluble marker to draw parallel lines as channel quilting stitching guides; and treat these two layers as one where channel-quilted fabric is referenced.

Note: This method is best suited to smaller pieces of fabric, but will work with larger ones as well.

■ Cut matching rectangles of the print fabric and the channel-quilted fabric for each required piece, cutting the rectangles slightly larger than the actual patterns to compensate for the slight "shrinkage" that occurs during quilting (Figure 1).

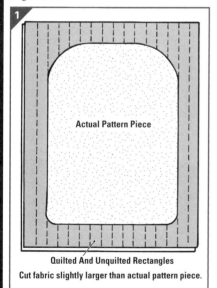

Quilted And Unquilted Rectangles
Cut fabric slightly larger than actual pattern piece.

■ Quilt the two fabric layers together following the steps below:

• Working on a large flat surface and with the fabrics wrong sides together, smooth the printed fabric on top of the quilted fabric; press lightly to remove any wrinkles.
• Turn the fabrics so the quilted side is up; make sure the bottom layer is flat and smooth.
• Using size No. 1 safety pins, pin the fabrics together, spacing the pins no more than 4" apart and placing them in between the channel quilting lines (Figure 2).

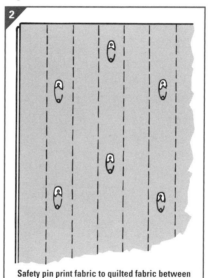

Safety pin print fabric to quilted fabric between channel stitching.

• Roll the prepared fabric into a cylinder parallel with the channel stitching lines (Figure 3). If you're working with a large fabric rectangle, clamp each cylinder end with a clothespin to temporarily secure it.
• Position the rolled fabric under the machine arm, quilting side up, and stitch on top of the original (or drawn) channel quilting lines, unrolling the cylinder to the next line until all lines have been stitched (Figure 4).

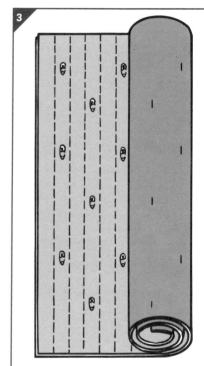

Roll fabric into cylinder parallel with channel stitching.

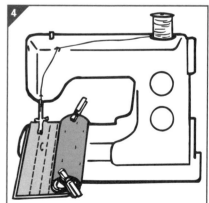

With cylinder under machine arm, stitch along channel-quilted lines, unrolling cylinder until all rows are stitched.

CHAPTER 3

SEW-SPOOKY COSTUMING

Halloween is a time for dress-up, sweet treats and bewitching fun, and although always a favorite for kids, this holiday is special for mom, too, as she creates the magic of the holiday with pudgy pumpkins, little devils, friendly witches, jolly jesters...all sewn to perfection with her mystical touch. As screams of excitement (and fright!) fill this haunted evening of festivities, your child will feel extra special donning a unique costume made just for him or her.

We have hopefully tickled your fancy with a host of darling—and daring—costuming options (refer to the photos on pages 10 and 11) that will inspire you and your child to dream and scheme to make just the right ensemble, complete with correct embellishments, for a night to remember.

These costumes serve as just-for-fun dress-up clothes, too, and can be used year-round for playtime and make-believe. They might also fit the bill for some of your child's other activities: parades, school plays, dance recitals and more.

You'll find that some of the costuming articles are more explicit than others, relating to you quite specific steps, patterns, etc., for creating the designs, but don't let the less detail-specific stories deter you. We have included these articles, featuring very simple-to-make costumes, as inspirational pieces—so you can let your creativity flow, your imagination roam and involve your child in these enterprising and sometimes unconventional projects.

Be sure to enjoy your options. Some of the costumes require just a common sweatsuit right out of your child's closet to be embellished with basted-on felt appliqués. Others encourage more elaborate sewing and take advantage of the bevy of Halloween prints available. However, we have focused on keeping all the designs very simple and easy to sew— even for beginners. So, go ahead and take the plunge into sewing boo-tiful Halloween costumes— there's no trick to creating these festive ensembles, and your treat will come in the form of a child's sparkling smile when he or she wears a costume of mom's own special brew. ❏

or photo
lished projects
on page 10

terror-ific!

If the thought of sewing a batch of Halloween costumes for anxious little trick-or-treaters this year gives you a bad case of the "frights," you're in for a surprise. You don't have to spend a fortune on materials or invest a lot of sewing time to come up with quick disguises to thrill even your choosiest goblin. With a little ingenuity and fabrics and trims from your stash, you can transfer items you have on hand into wild and wacky costumes, then wave your wand and return them to their original purpose with no one the wiser.

GATHER YOUR RESOURCES

If you and your kids are fresh out of ideas for "what to be this Halloween," check out the kids' coloring and comic books and Saturday morning cartoons for some great characters to copy. Storybooks and costume history books are other good resources.

To avoid a lot of sewing, sort out your child's exercise gear—leotards and tights, headbands, jogging suits, hooded sweatshirts and pull-on pants can all be put to work as the base for creative costumes. One-piece, footed sleepers and long underwear are other possibilities. Using activewear and nightwear as a costume base has another advantage: Your little spooks will stay toasty warm while collecting their goodies door-to-door. Sneakers and slippers can be embellished for fanciful footwear. And to keep ears and other headgear in place, cover a plastic headband with fabric (Figure 1), then hand sew additions in place.

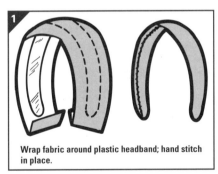

Wrap fabric around plastic headband; hand stitch in place.

COSTUME IDEAS

■ Turn your little "punkin" into a pumpkin in bright orange sweats by adding black felt appliqués to the sweatshirt front for the jack-o-lantern face. To make the appliqués removable, baste them in place. Make a simple "hat" from orange felt with a green felt stem stuffed with fiberfill, then attach it to a cloth-covered headband. For a more realistic pumpkin look on an older child, stuff an oversized shirt with pillows or fiberfill, then belt or tie the shirt lower edge to hold everything in place over matching orange sweats, tights or leggings.

■ Turn a black leotard and tights (or unitard) into a life-size skeleton with white felt appliqués cut in the shape of ribs, pelvic, arm and leg bones. The most effective and easiest way to apply these appliqués is to glue-baste them in place (using a temporary-holding glue for speedy removal after Halloween) while the child is wearing the leotard or unitard. For hands, add bony finger appliqués to black gloves, for feet add bony foot and toe appliqués to black shoes, sneakers or ballet slippers. For the skull, pull a white nylon stocking over the head. If your goblin won't stand still for attaching the skeleton appliqués, machine baste the appliqués to black sweats—not quite as "life"-like, but still to the point.

■ Ballerinas and fairy godmothers are easy to contrive from pink tights and leotards.

Make a tutu by gathering nylon netting or tulle and attaching it to a ribbon long enough to fit around the waist and tie in a bow. For ballet slippers, lace grosgrain ribbon, crisscross-style, up the leg, then have the little prima ballerina wear flat shoes or slippers (Figure 2). Add an oversized glittery lamé or shiny ribbon bow to the headband.

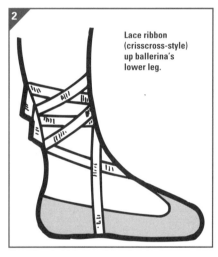

Lace ribbon (crisscross-style) up ballerina's lower leg.

For a fairy godmother, use the same tutu and make a magic wand: Cut two star shapes from a scrap of silvery metallic fabric. Wrong sides together, stitch close to the edge, leaving an opening. Insert a dowel or long-handled wooden spoon into the opening (Figure 3), stuff with a bit of fiberfill and sew the opening closed around the "wand." Add glittery rhinestones or sequins to the leotard neckline with a few hand stitches.

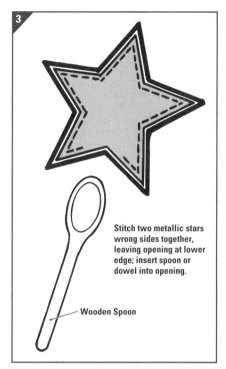

Stitch two metallic stars wrong sides together, leaving opening at lower edge; insert spoon or dowel into opening.

Wooden Spoon

■ Turn a little boy into his favorite weight lifter or TV wrestler using two large long-sleeved T-shirts. Slip an old throwaway T-shirt inside an outer shirt and outline muscle shapes through both layers with extra long basting stitches you can remove easily later. On the inside, carefully cut a slit in the inner (throwaway) shirt *only* and stuff the muscles with fiberfill (Figure 4). Have him wear this with tights, swimming briefs and one of Dad's belts for the weight-lifting belt.

For a barbell weight, use silver spray paint on a discarded cardboard tube and add red spray-painted cardboard o Styrofoam® disks at the end for "weights."

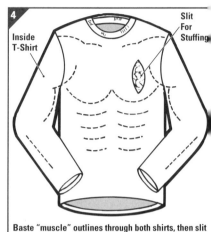

Inside T-Shirt

Slit For Stuffing

Baste "muscle" outlines through both shirts, then slit inner shirt at "muscle" areas and stuff with fiberfill.

■ Drum majors and majorette are easy to improvise, beginning with dark-colored o white sweats. Baste gol middy braid across the front o a sweatshirt in graduate lengths and add a gold butto to the end of each length Shape the hat from cardboar covered with felt and trimmed with braid and a feather. Add baton and some whit "slouch" socks and sneaker and he'll be ready to face th music in style.

olor photo
finished projects
on page 11

halloween in a hurry

Readily available in a variety of colors, children's sweat-suits are the perfect canvas for creating a whole range of easy-to-make (and wear!) Halloween costumes. The most successful sweatsuit conversions are simple looks, devoid of intricate sewing details; instead the best costumes rely on an imaginative mix of fabric and color, often supplemented with fused-on appliqués and fabric paint. Where appropriate, face makeup can add the perfect finishing touch.

IMAGINATIVE OPTIONS

For inspiration, look to the creatures of the forest, from ferocious lions to cuddly bunnies. Consider traditional Halloween themes or your child's favorite characters.

Still more ideas are no farther away than the kitchen cupboard. A well-recognized canned or bottled product with clean, easily identifiable graphics—such as Hershey's cocoa, Heinz ketchup or Campbell's soup can be re-created with simple appliqués and fabric paint.

Here we share two ideas to get you started on costumes for kids of all ages. And because the details on these fun-to-make designs are easy to remove, these costumes can be quickly converted back to everyday wear.

BASHFUL BUNNY

A hooded sweatshirt is the starting point for a lovable bunny, complete with floppy ears and a fluffy tail.

MATERIALS

• Hooded sweatshirt in white or pastel color

• ½ yard of pastel (for white bunny) or white (for pastel bunny) terry cloth

• ½ yard of a coordinating cotton print

• One skein of white rug yarn

• 2½"x4" cardboard rectangle

• Pattern tracing cloth

PREPARATION/CUTTING

Note: Use ⅝"-wide seam allowances unless otherwise indicated.

■ Enlarge the ear pattern in Figure 1 and cut two from the cotton print for outer ears, two from the terry cloth for inner ears.

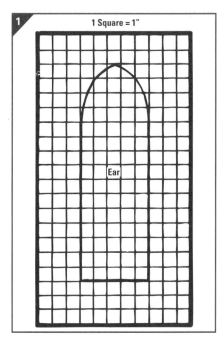

1   1 Square = 1"

Ear

■ Right sides together, stitch an outer ear to an inner ear, leaving the lower edges open. Trim the seams, clip the curves and turn the ear right side out (Figure 2, page 44).

Repeat with the remaining inner and outer ears.

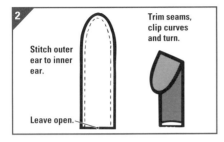

Stitch outer ear to inner ear.

Trim seams, clip curves and turn.

Leave open.

■ To position the ears:

• Have your child try on the sweatshirt and pin-mark the upper ear placement; remove the sweatshirt.

• Make a small tuck at the unfinished end of each ear so the end measures 2½" across.

• Turn under ¾" at the unfinished end of each ear toward the inner ear (terry cloth side) and hand tack one ear fold at a pin-marked ear location (Figure 3). *Note:* When the ear flops down, the unfinished end will be covered.

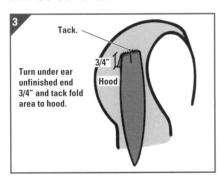

Tack.

Turn under ear unfinished end 3/4" and tack fold area to hood.

3/4"

Hood

■ Pin or tape a piece of pattern tracing cloth to the sweatshirt front; on the tracing cloth, draw a stomach patch oval that extends from the neckline ribbing to the sweatshirt lower edge ribbing and is wide enough to cover the wearer's actual body width (Figure 4);

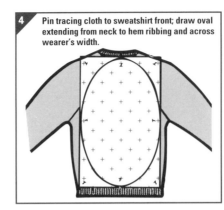

Pin tracing cloth to sweatshirt front; draw oval extending from neck to hem ribbing and across wearer's width.

add ⅝" seam allowances and cut one stomach patch from the terry cloth.

■ Press under the stomach patch seam allowances ⅝" or serge-finish the stomach patch raw edges using matching decorative thread and a balanced 3-thread stitch. Pin and edgestitch or baste (for easy removal) the stomach patch over the sweatshirt front.

■ To make the neck bow:

• Cut four 4"x 35" strips from the remaining print fabric.

• Right sides together, stitch two strips together end to end to form a 4"x 68¾" strip; repeat with the remaining two strips.

• Right sides together and raw edges even, stitch the strips together in a ¼" seam, leaving an opening for turning (Figure 5). Turn the resulting tube right side out, press and slipstitch the opening closed. *Note:* For a quick serger finish, pin the two strips wrong sides together and serge around all edges using matching decorative

thread and a balanced 3-thread stitch.

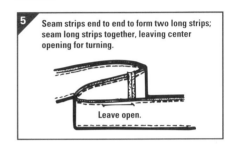

Seam strips end to end to form two long strips; seam long strips together, leaving center opening for turning.

Leave open.

■ To make the tail:

• Cut an 8" length of yarn.

• Wind the remaining yarn around the cardboard rectangle approximately 150 times. Run the 8" length of yarn under all the loops at one cardboard edge and tie it tightly around the loops.

• Cut through all the yarn loops at the opposite cardboard rectangle edge to create a pompom tail (Figure 6).

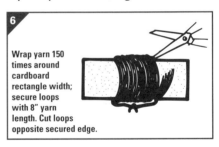

Wrap yarn 150 times around cardboard rectangle width; secure loops with 8" yarn length. Cut loops opposite secured edge.

• Tack the pompom tail in place at the center back of the sweatpants seat.

■ To complete the costume, have your child put on the "sweats" with the hood up and the hood drawstring pulled taut around the face and tied; tie the bow around the neck over the hood. If desired, use black eyeliner pencil to draw a small round circle at the tip of the child's nose and three whiskers on each cheek.

JOLLY JESTER

This court jester is a sprightly study in contrasts that's perfect for energetic youngsters.

MATERIALS

- Crew-neck sweatshirt and sweatpants in contrasting colors
- Coordinating beret or knitted cap
- ½ yard each of two contrasting colors of felt
- 16 jingle bells
- Pattern tracing cloth

PREPARATION/CUTTING

■ On pattern tracing cloth, draw a triangle with a 5"-wide base and 10"-tall apex (Figure 7); using the pattern, cut 14 felt triangles (seven from each felt color).

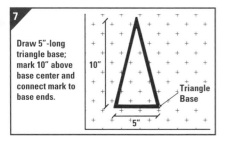

7 Draw 5"-long triangle base; mark 10" above base center and connect mark to base ends.

10"

Triangle Base

5"

■ Pin eight triangles (four of each color) around the sweatshirt neck edge, just below the ribbed neckline band, arranging them so the colors alternate and the bases overlap

slightly (Figure 8); tack each triangle in place at the base center and corners.

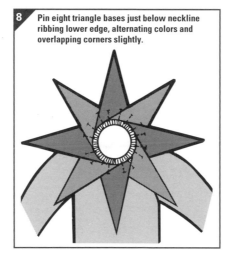

8 Pin eight triangle bases just below neckline ribbing lower edge, alternating colors and overlapping corners slightly.

■ Alternating the colors and making a small tuck at each base to give it shape, pin the remaining six triangles with their bases overlapping at the center of the cap or beret (Figure 9); hand tack each triangle at the base center and edges.

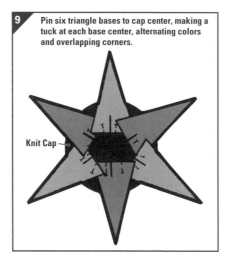

9 Pin six triangle bases to cap center, making a tuck at each base center, alternating colors and overlapping corners.

Knit Cap

■ From one of the felt scraps, cut a starburst shape just large enough to cover the opening created at the center of the triangle bases and tack or glue it in place at the cap top (Figure 10).

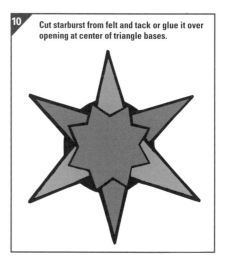

10 Cut starburst from felt and tack or glue it over opening at center of triangle bases.

■ Cut the remaining felt into small squares, circles and/or triangles; fuse, glue or, for easy removal, machine baste them in place randomly on the sweats, using pieces that contrast each half.

■ Hand stitch a jingle bell to the tip of each felt triangle and, if desired, glue one near the tip of each shoe (perhaps two different-colored, slip-on tennis shoes) to be worn with the costume. ❏

— KID-BITS —

Girls from the Victorian era wore corsets from early childhood through adulthood.

— POCKETS PERFECT! —

Nothing is more frustrating for your child (and you!) than stuffing his or her pockets with life's essentials, only to find the pocket corners can't take the strain. To avoid these embarrassing tears, try one of the following simple reinforcement techniques:

■ Use a narrow, closely spaced zigzag stitch when stitching the first ½" of each pocket upper corner in place (Figure 1). *Note:* This technique is commonly used to reinforce pockets on ready-to-wear children's clothing.

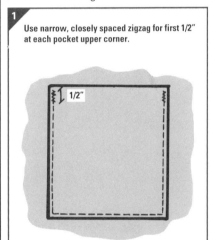

1
Use narrow, closely spaced zigzag for first 1/2" at each pocket upper corner.

■ Stitch small, identical triangles at each pocket upper corner (Figure 2), bartacking to anchor the stitching or bringing the thread ends through to the garment wrong side and tying them off. *Note:* This method is frequently used on the pockets of men's tailored shirts.

■ Backstitch for ½" along each side of the pocket stitching at each pocket upper corner (Figure 3), bringing the thread ends through to the garment wrong side and tying them off.

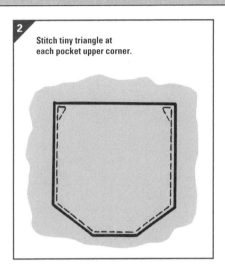

2
Stitch tiny triangle at each pocket upper corner.

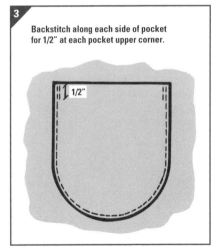

3
Backstitch along each side of pocket for 1/2" at each pocket upper corner.

■ Use diagonal bartacks, created with narrow, closely spaced zigzag stitches, to reinforce each pocket upper corner on Western-look designs (Figure 4).

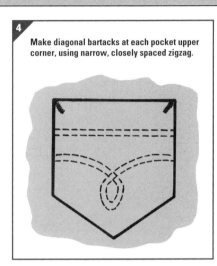

4
Make diagonal bartacks at each pocket upper corner, using narrow, closely spaced zigzag.

■ When sewing lightweight fabrics, place a small patch of fabric or fusible interfacing behind the reinforcement stitching for additional strength (Figure 5), then reinforce the area with one of the above options.

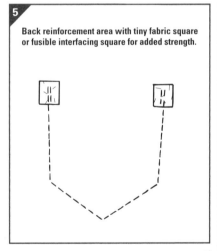

5
Back reinforcement area with tiny fabric square or fusible interfacing square for added strength.

r photo
ished project
on page 11

devil duty

So, it's time to start thinking about Halloween again and what to sew or your own little goblin. If you have just a bit of time, you can forget the notion of surrendering to an expensive, ordinary, yet convenient costume from the local five and dime. This costume promises swift yet creative results. And besides stitching up quickly, it requires minimal materials—you probably have everything you need in your stash and in your child's closet—and will be useful after that infamous evening of Halloween magic.

A sewn or ready-made sweatsuit is the base of this costume, your creativity and imagination the key to its success.

MATERIALS

- Red hooded sweatshirt and sweatpants or fabric and pattern to sew both
- Three 9"x12" pieces of red felt
- Two pipe cleaners
- Scraps of polyester fiberfill
- Matching thread
- Black or white fabric paint

CONSTRUCTION

■ If you plan to sew the sweatshirt and sweatpants, complete each before beginning.

■ Enlarge the patterns in Figure 1 and cut four horns and two tail ends from red felt. Also, cut two 2"x10" tail rectangles from red felt.

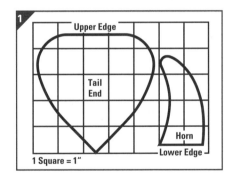

1
Upper Edge
Tail End
Horn
Lower Edge
1 Square = 1"

■ Raw edges matching, stitch two horns together in a ¼" seam, leaving the lower edge open; repeat with the remaining two horns and two tail ends, leaving a 2"-long opening along the tail end's upper edge. Carefully trim each

seam allowance to a scant ⅛". Raw edges matching, stitch the 2"x10" rectangles together along all edges; trim the seam allowances to a scant ⅛".

■ Insert one pipe cleaner into each horn lower edge opening, then trim each pipe cleaner ½" shorter than the horns.

■ Stuff the horns and tail end firmly and evenly with fiberfill to within ½" of each unstitched edge, using the eraser end of a pencil to maneuver fiberfill into the curves and points.

■ Insert ½" of one short end of the tail into the tail end opening, then finish the tail end stitching (Figure 2).

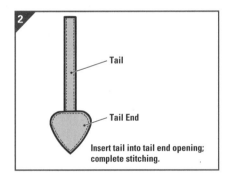

2
Tail
Tail End
Insert tail into tail end opening; complete stitching.

■ Hand stitch the remaining short end of the tail to the sweatshirt waistband ribbing at the center back.

■ Make a 4"-long slash across the crown on the sweatshirt hood 2" to 3" from the face opening (Figure 3, page 48).

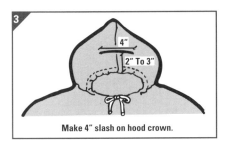

Make 4" slash on hood crown.

■ From the hood right side, insert each horn lower edge into the hood slashed opening, positioning one horn at each end of the slash (about 2" apart) and the horn points facing each other; pin in place.

■ Working from the hood wrong side, pin the slashed opening back together and stitch across it with a very narrow seam, tapering to the ends to avoid obvious points. *Note:* Use a long basting stitch, backstitching at each end, so you can easily remove the horns and stitch the slash closed after Halloween, if desired.

■ Bend the pipe cleaner in each horn to the desired position.

■ Transfer the lettering "I'm A Little Devil" to the sweatshirt front, using fabric paints (Figure 4).

Add lettering to sweatshirt front with fabric paints.

— BRACE YOURSELF! —

Cord bracelets—they're all the rage with kids these days. Incredibly popular year-round, this design trend is especially prevalent for kids on the beach. Make them in the bright brights to match your child's swimsuit or Ts. The bracelets can be worn on the wrist and ankles or as ponytail holders—and they're easy to make!

You'll need the following: One 1½"x15" fabric strip (cut on the bias for wovens, on the crossgrain for knits); two or three 1-yard pieces of washable yarn to use as cording; and two ½"-diameter wooden macrame beads (with ¼"-diameter holes).

To make each cord bracelet:

■ Fold the fabric in half lengthwise, right sides together, over one-half of the yarn pieces' length. Stitch across the fabric end at the yarn center.

■ Using a zipper foot, stitch the strip's long edges close to the yarn; trim the fabric close to the stitching line (Figure 1).

■ To turn the tube right side out, hold the yarn end extending from the covered end and work the fabric over the uncovered yarn (Figure 2).

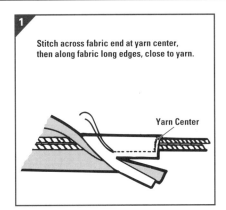

Stitch across fabric end at yarn center, then along fabric long edges, close to yarn.

Yarn Center

To turn tube, hold yarn at covered end and work tube over uncovered end.

Yarn Center

■ Cut off the extra yarn.
■ Slip both beads onto the tube.
■ Knot one tube end; insert the other end through the beads (Figure 3).

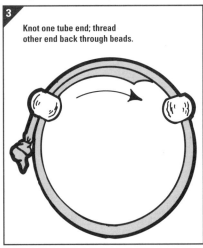

Knot one tube end; thread other end back through beads.

■ Pull the ends to adjust the bracelet fit. Trim any excess tube.
■ Knot the remaining tube end. ❑

bewitching capers

This witch is just a little bit scary, but oh-so-chic, in her authentic-looking hat and cape accented with a snappy Halloween print. The cape is reversible, so you can choose to entertain a more serious (black) or light-hearted (print) Halloween witch for trick-or-treating or holiday festivities.

MATERIALS

- 2½ yards of 45"-wide cotton or cotton-blend black fabric
- 2½ yards of 45"-wide cotton or cotton-blend Halloween print fabric
- 1¼ yards of 19"-wide buckram
- 2½ yards of 18"-wide fusible transfer web
- ¼ yard of ¼"-wide black elastic
- Pattern tracing cloth
- Matching thread
- White craft glue or hot glue gun
- Seam sealant, such as Fray Check™

WITCH'S HAT CONSTRUCTION

■ Determine the hat's necessary base measurement by measuring the child's head circumference and adding 1".

■ Cut a piece of buckram equal in length to the base measurement. Mark the center along one lengthwise edge, then mark ½" on either side of the center mark, as shown in Figure 1.

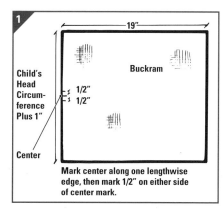

Mark center along one lengthwise edge, then mark 1/2" on either side of center mark.

■ Draw a diagonal line from each ½" marking to an opposite corner, then trim along these lines to create a blunt-tipped triangle for the hat cone foundation (Figure 2).

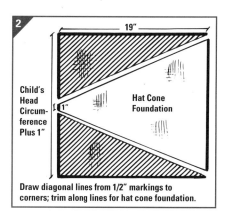

Draw diagonal lines from 1/2" markings to corners; trim along lines for hat cone foundation.

■ Cut a black and a print blunt-tipped fabric triangle, each approximately 1" larger than the hat cone foundation.

■ Apply fusible transfer web to both sides of the hat cone foundation (buckram).

■ Remove one layer of the fusible transfer web backing paper and fuse this side of the hat cone foundation to the black triangle wrong side; trim off the excess fabric.

Repeat to fuse the other side of the hat cone foundation to the print triangle wrong side; trim off the excess fabric.

■ Apply a ¾"-wide strip of fusible transfer web to one diagonal edge of the hat cone foundation on the print side (Figure 3, page 50). Remove the fusible transfer web paper backing.

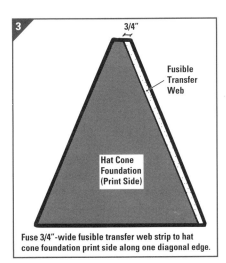

Fuse 3/4"-wide fusible transfer web strip to hat cone foundation print side along one diagonal edge.

■ Roll the hat cone foundation into a cone, black side out, overlapping the diagonal edges ¾"; fuse this edge in place. *Note:* To secure the cone for fusing, staple the overlapped edges together at the base and pin them together at the tip, then stuff cotton batting into the tip and fuse over a sleeve board or seam roll; reshape the tip with your fingers while it is still damp from fusing.

■ Flatten the hat cone at the base area, then trim the back (seamed) edge to match the front edge (Figure 4). Apply seam sealant to the cut edges to prevent fraying.

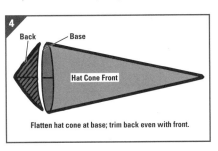

Flatten hat cone at base; trim back even with front.

■ Place the hat cone on the child's head, centering the cone seam at the back of the child's head, and pin the elastic to fit comfortably under the chin; machine stitch the elastic ends in place on the hat cone inside (print side).

■ Cut a 19"-diameter circle from buckram for the hat brim.

■ Measure the hat cone diameter at the base; on pattern tracing cloth, draw an inner circle pattern this diameter. Center the inner circle pattern on the 19"-diameter buckram circle and cut out along the pattern outline for the hat brim inner circle (Figure 5).

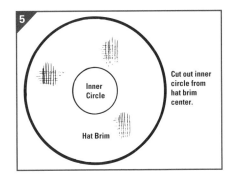

Cut out inner circle from hat brim center.

Inner Circle

Hat Brim

■ Cut a black and a print fabric circle 1" larger than the hat brim; do not cut out the inner circle.

■ Apply fusible transfer web to both sides of the buckram hat brim, cutting out the inner circle.

■ Remove one layer of the fusible transfer web backing paper and fuse this side of the brim to the black fabric circle wrong side; trim off the excess

fabric along the outer edges only.

Repeat to fuse the other side of the buckram brim to the print fabric circle wrong side; trim off the excess fabric along the outer edges only and apply seam sealant to the outer edges to prevent fraying.

■ Using the pattern created above, cut another inner circle pattern 1" smaller in diameter than the original inner circle pattern. Center this new pattern on the hat brim and beginning at the inner circle center, cut out this inner circle through all layers. Clip to the buckram brim inner circle in 1" intervals (Figure 6).

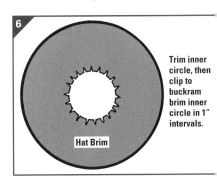

Trim inner circle, then clip to buckram brim inner circle in 1" intervals.

Hat Brim

■ Working from the hat base printed side, insert the hat cone pointed end through the hat base inner circle, sliding the brim down to the cone base; the inner circle notches should extend toward the cone point (Figure 7, page 51). Glue the base in place.

■ Cut a 2"-wide printed fabric strip 2" longer than the hat cone base diameter for the hat band.

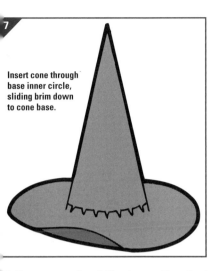

Insert cone through base inner circle, sliding brim down to cone base.

■ Press under ½" along the hat band long and short edges, then glue the band in place wrong side down along the hat cone base area, overlapping the ends 1" and concealing the brim notches (Figure 8).

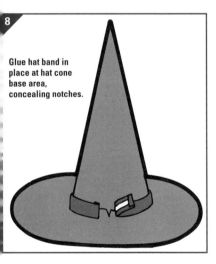

Glue hat band in place at hat cone base area, concealing notches.

WITCH'S CAPE CONSTRUCTION

Note: Use ⅝" seam allowances throughout.

■ Enlarge the patterns in Figure 9, adjusting the length as necessary for the child. Cut two fronts and two backs from the black solid fabric for the cape and two fronts and two backs from the print fabric for the cape lining. Transfer the arm opening markings to each piece.

■ Right sides together, stitch the cape backs together along the center back seam, then stitch the cape back to the cape fronts along the side seams, leaving an opening between the arm opening markings at each side seam. Press the seams open.

Repeat for the cape lining.

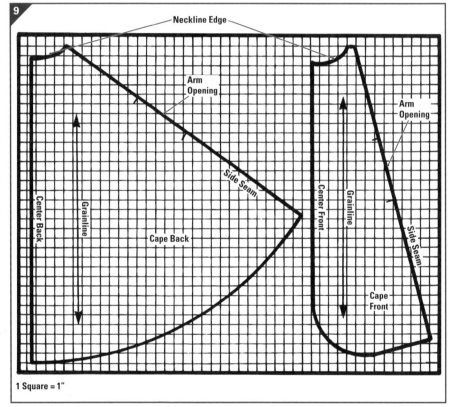

1 Square = 1"

■ Right sides together, stitch the cape to the cape lining along the outer edges, *except* the neckline edge. Trim the seam, clip the curved edges and turn the cape right side out through the neckline opening. Press.

■ Baste the seam allowances together along the neckline edge, then topstitch ⅜" from all outer edges, including the neckline edge.

■ Pin the cape to the cape lining at the arm openings, then topstitch around the arm openings ¼" from edges (Figure 10).

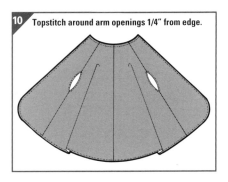

10 Topstitch around arm openings 1/4" from edge.

■ From the remaining print fabric, cut and piece enough 2"-wide bias strips to form one 60"-long strip.

■ Use the bias binding to encase the cape neckline edge, centering the binding on the neckline and allowing the ends to extend beyond the neckline for ties (Figure 11). *Note:* See "Applying Bias Binding" on page 83 for instructions on applying bias binding.

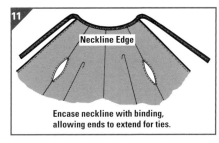

11   Neckline Edge

Encase neckline with binding, allowing ends to extend for ties.

❑

— BOO! —

Halloween, always a favorite holiday, has become a major event each year—for everyone from small children anticipating trick-or-treating to their parents hosting costume parties for little spooks' sew-scary antics. Take the following costume safety tips seriously so your child will have the happiest, safest Halloween possible:

■ Be sure costumes, including beards, wigs and masks, are flame-resistant.

■ Avoid oversized or awkward costumes that cause your child difficulty in walking, obscure his or her vision or restrict normal breathing.

■ If your child must wear a mask (the safest costumes do not include masks), be sure it fits well and is secure.

■ Instead of masks, decorate your child's face with special face paints or makeup to portray a character.

■ For after-dark trick-or-treating, make sure your child is visible to motorists by embellishing his or her costume or goody bag with reflective trim or glow-in-the-dark fabrics and having the child carry a flashlight.   ❑

KIDS'-ROOM CAPERS

In a child's eyes, his or her bedroom is generally the most important room in the house. This is the one area that's the child's very own, and how it's decorated should be as much of a reflection on that child's personality as possible.

Whether you're sewing a complete nursery ensemble for the new baby in your life or some clever accents for your 10-year-old's own private haven, careful planning and lots of creativity will contribute to your success.

"Babes In Nurseryland" gives you a head start on preparing for baby's arrival, offering detailed instructions for everything from crib sheets to bumper pads to a diaper stacker. The story focuses on using sheets for the fabric medium. It's an economical way to outfit a nursery in true decorator fashion—especially when you can find sheets to suit your theme at white sales or discount outlet stores. You can adapt the instructions for use with fabric, too, if you'd just like to take advantage of the project how-tos.

As you choose you own nursery formula (or you're devising a plan for an older child's room), keep in mind that the more expensive, permanent background purchases—floor and wall treatments—should be neutral, "age"-less selections. These can be jazzed up (and updated later) with the changeables—window treatments, crib or bed accessories and room accents. That's welcome news to creative home-sewers who can use decorator sheets or precious juvenile fabrics to sew room accessories far superior to their ready-made counterparts.

If you're sewing for older kids, encourage them to assist you in fabric selections, so they'll be pleased and proud to display your work in their own room. "Hand-Print Keepsake" involves the child (or children) even more by allowing them to give a wall quilt their own personal "touch" with their actual handprints transferred to the quilt with fabric paints.

This simple project will be a special memento for generations to come.

These projects are meant to motivate you to sew for your little one's nursery or bedroom, while brightly colored fabrics (and fabric paints!) will inspire the imagination. Use the instructions as guidelines,

then embellish to your heart's content!

Most of all, enjoy this sewing endeavor, knowing when those bright eyes open each morning, your child will see your loving stitches as a sign of your special bond.

babes in nurseryland

Department store displays and magazine layouts have shown us beautiful but costly ways to decorate a nursery. Using a little know-how and the designer sheets of your choice, you, too, can create a showcase nursery—for less than $60, if you find the sheets on sale.

Watch for white sales and purchase twin flat sheets, as they're usually the least expensive and offer the most for your money. If the nursery has a wide window, splurge on a full or queen size sheet for the window treatment.

CRIB SHEETS

MATERIALS

• One twin flat sheet (this will yield two fitted crib sheets)

• ⅜"-wide elastic measuring twice the mattress circumference

• Air-soluble marker

• Matching thread

MEASURING/CUTTING

Note: Make all markings between the sheet's hemmed edges. If you'll be using a mattress pad, place the pad on the mattress before measuring.

■ Take the following mattress measurements: total width (A), which includes the mattress width, plus twice the depth, plus 2"; and total length (B), which includes the mattress length, plus twice the depth, plus 2" (Figure 1).

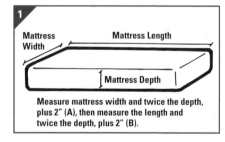

Mark two crib sheets on flat sheet.

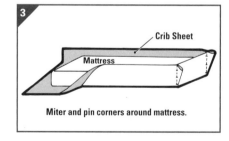

Measure mattress width and twice the depth, plus 2" (A), then measure the length and twice the depth, plus 2" (B).

■ Using the air-soluble marker and the total width and length measurements determined above, mark two crib sheets on the flat sheet (Figure 2).

■ Cut out the sheets along the marked lines.

CONSTRUCTION

■ Place one sheet right side up and center the crib mattress on top of it.

■ Miter and pin the corners around the mattress, allowing enough ease to remove the sheet (Figure 3).

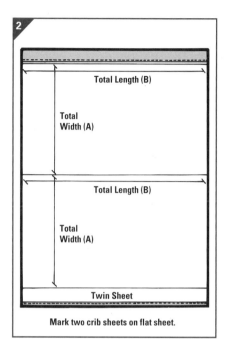

Miter and pin corners around mattress.

■ Gently remove the mattress and machine stitch the sheet corners, using the pins as seam guides (Figure 4, page 56). Trim excess fabric. Serge or overcast the seam edges for additional strength.

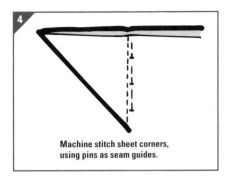

Machine stitch sheet corners, using pins as seam guides.

■ Measure the sheet opening circumference (Figure 5).

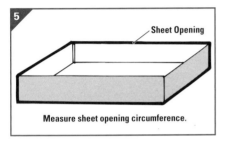

Measure sheet opening circumference.

■ Cut a length of ⅜"-wide elastic 7" shorter than the sheet opening circumference.

■ Overlap the elastic ends ½" and stitch. *Note:* The elastic should now be 8" shorter than the sheet opening.

■ Divide the elastic and the sheet opening raw edge into quarters and pin-mark each quarter point.

■ Match the elastic pin-marks to the sheet pin-marks on the sheet wrong side. Stitch the elastic in place using a zigzag, three-step zigzag or serger stitch, stretching the elastic to fit and keeping the elastic and sheet opening edges even.

BUMPER PAD

Note: The following materials and instructions will yield a bumper pad to fit a standard 27"x52" crib.

MATERIALS

• One twin flat sheet (this will yield a standard-sized bumper pad, plus enough fabric to cover a changing table pad)

• 2¼ yards of ⅜"-wide ribbon

• Two 22"-long nylon zippers

• Two 36"-long nylon zippers

• Air-soluble marker

• Matching thread

• Two 25"x8"x1" strips of foam

• Two 50"x8"x1" strips of foam

• Two 25"x19" strips of ⅝"-thick batting

• Two 50"x19" strips of ⅝"-thick batting

• Approximately 10 yards of kitchen plastic wrap

MEASURING/MARKING

Note: Make all markings between the sheet's hemmed edges.

■ Cut four 9½"x80" strips from the sheet for the bumper pad panels.

■ Right sides together, join the 9½" edges of two panels in a ½" seam, forming one long panel (Figure 6); repeat with the remaining two panels. Press the seams open.

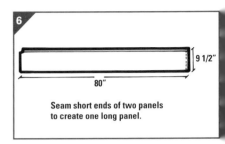

9 1/2"

80"

Seam short ends of two panels to create one long panel.

■ Mark the zipper placements along the long edges of each panel as shown Figure 7, page 57.

■ Right sides together, join the panels together along one long edge in a 1" seam, machine basting between the 22" and 36" zipper placement markings (Figure 8, page 57). Press the seam open.

■ Insert the zippers using a centered application.

■ Right sides together and raw edges even, stitch each panel short end in a ½" seam (Figure 9, page 57).

■ If desired, attach a ruffle to one long edge of the panel, with right sides together and raw edges even. *Note:* See "Ruffling Made Easy" on page 103 for instructions on creating ruffling.

■ Right sides together, stitch the remaining panel long edges in a ½" seam (Figure 10, page 57). *Note:* If you attached the optional ruffle, use the ruffle stitching line as a guide.

■ Open the 36" zipper nearest the panel center seam, turn the pad right side out and press.

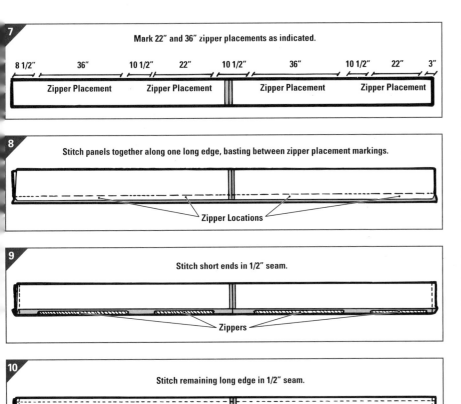

7

Mark 22" and 36" zipper placements as indicated.

| 8 1/2" | 36" | 10 1/2" | 22" | 10 1/2" | 36" | 10 1/2" | 22" | 3" |

Zipper Placement   Zipper Placement   Zipper Placement   Zipper Placement

8

Stitch panels together along one long edge, basting between zipper placement markings.

Zipper Locations

9

Stitch short ends in 1/2" seam.

Zippers

10

Stitch remaining long edge in 1/2" seam.

■ Stitch through both thicknesses of the panel as follows: at the center seam (stitch in the ditch); 52" to the right of the center seam; and 27" to the left of the center seam as shown in Figure 11.

■ Cut the ribbon into four 20"-long ties; apply seam sealant

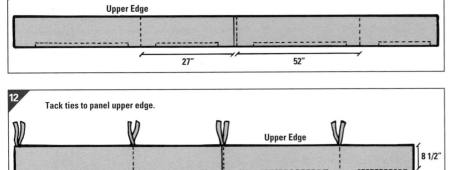

11

Topstitch or stitch in the ditch to form padding sections.

Upper Edge

27"   52"

12

Tack ties to panel upper edge.

Upper Edge

8 1/2"

to the end of each to prevent raveling. Tack the center of each ribbon tie to the upper, unzipped edge of the panel as shown in Figure 12. *Note:* If you added a ruffle, tack the ribbons behind it.

■ To make the bumper pad cover filler:

• Wrap each foam strip firmly with its respective batting strip; catchstitch the batting by hand to secure (Figure 13).

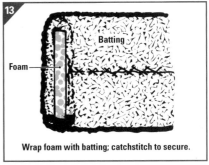

13

Batting

Foam

Wrap foam with batting; catchstitch to secure.

• Beginning at one end of the batting-wrapped foam, wrap the plastic wrap around the batting, overlapping wraps to completely encase it. Catchstitch the plastic wrap in place to secure (Figure 14).

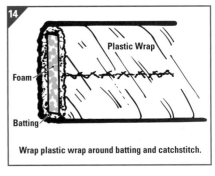

14

Plastic Wrap

Foam

Batting

Wrap plastic wrap around batting and catchstitch.

■ Through the zipper openings, insert one 25" piece of

wrapped foam into each 27" panel section, one 50" piece of wrapped foam into each 52" panel section.

■ Slipstitch the padded panel together along the finished 8½" edges. Insert the bumper pad into the crib, ribbon ties up, and secure the ribbon ties to the crib spindles.

DIAPER STACKER

MATERIALS

- One twin flat sheet
- 2 yards of extra-wide bias tape
- Padded hanger
- Air-soluble marker
- Tissue paper
- 11"x15" piece of heavy cardboard

MEASURING/CUTTING

Note: Make all markings between the sheet's hemmed edges.

■ Cut the following pieces from the sheet: two 15"x26" stacker fronts; one 26"x28" stacker back; and one 3½"x36" ruffle (optional).

■ Make a hanger yoke pattern using the hanger as a guide, as shown in Figure 15.

■ Cut two hanger yokes from the sheet fabric.

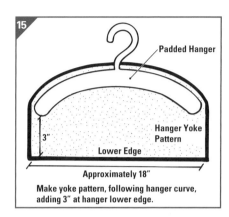

Make yoke pattern, following hanger curve, adding 3" at hanger lower edge.

CONSTRUCTION

■ Press under ½", then ½" again along one 26" edge of each front piece; topstitch in place for the center fronts (Figure 16).

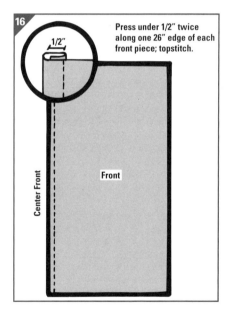

Press under 1/2" twice along one 26" edge of each front piece; topstitch.

■ If desired, bind the center front edge of each front piece, using 1½"-wide strips of coordinating bias binding. *Note:* See "Applying Bias Binding" on page 83 for instructions on applying bias binding.

■ Right sides together and raw edges matching, stitch the fronts to the back at the side and lower edges in a ½" seam, pivoting at the corners. *Note:* The center fronts are *not* stitched together.

■ If desired, attach a ruffle to one yoke lower edge for the yoke front. *Note:* See "Ruffling Made Easy" on page 76 for instructions on creating ruffling.

■ Right sides together and raw edges matching, stitch the yoke front and back together in a ½" seam, leaving the lower edge open and leaving a 1" opening for the hanger hook as shown in Figure 17.

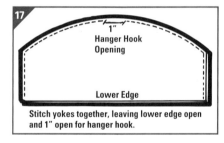

Stitch yokes together, leaving lower edge open and 1" open for hanger hook.

■ Turn the yoke right side out; mark the yoke center at the lower edge.

■ Right sides together, insert the yoke between the stacker front/back, with the yoke lower raw edges even with the stacker upper raw edges, matching centers (Figure 18, page 59). Pin each yoke raw edge to its respective stacker raw edge.

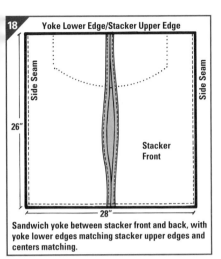

18 Yoke Lower Edge/Stacker Upper Edge

Side Seam

Side Seam

26"

Stacker Front

28"

Sandwich yoke between stacker front and back, with yoke lower edges matching stacker upper edges and centers matching.

■ Make two inverted pleats at each stacker side seam so the stacker upper edge matches the yoke lower edge (Figure 19).

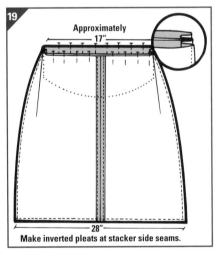

19 Approximately 17"

28"

Make inverted pleats at stacker side seams.

■ Stitch the yoke to the stacker in a ½" seam along the raw edges, securing the pleats.

■ Press all seams open.

■ To square the stacker bottom:

• Right sides together, lay the stacker lower edge seam over a side seam, forming a 90-degree angle.

• Measure on the seam 5½" from the corner point and draw a line perpendicular to the seam; stitch on this line (Figure 20). Repeat on the remaining side seam.

■ Turn the stacker right side out through the center front openings.

■ Cover the cardboard piece with excess fabric, hot gluing it in place. Insert this piece into the stacker, fabric side up, for the stacker bottom.

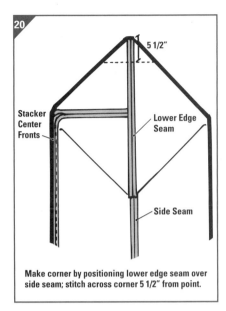

20 5 1/2"

Stacker Center Fronts

Lower Edge Seam

Side Seam

Make corner by positioning lower edge seam over side seam; stitch across corner 5 1/2" from point.

■ Insert the hanger through the center front openings, then the hanger hook through the hanger hook opening.

❑

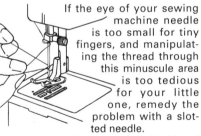

— THREADING TACTIC —

If the eye of your sewing machine needle is too small for tiny fingers, and manipulating the thread through this minuscule area is too tedious for your little one, remedy the problem with a slotted needle.

Available in European sizes 80, 90 and 100, this needle features a slot in the side of the eye. To thread, hold the thread strand firmly behind and in front of the needle and pass the thread along the needle shaft until it glides into the slot.

Note: Because the eye is slotted, this needle is more fragile than a standard needle of comparable size, so be sure the child is gentle when threading and handling it, and use it only on light- to mediumweight fabrics.

Check with your local sewing machine dealer to determine if this specialized needle is available to fit your machine. ❑

hand-printed keepsake

Whether it's the handiwork of one small fry, a friendship quilt "autographed" by the neighborhood kids or a family keepsake signed by siblings, this project is designed (and destined!) to intrigue budding artists.

One solid fabric and four coordinating prints form the base of this 36"-square wall hanging. Then sashing strips are fused in place to create the illusion of a pieced quilt. Machine quilting is the extra-easy touch.

MATERIALS

• 1 yard of 45"-wide solid-colored cotton fabric for the center panel (hand prints background fabric)

• 1½ yards of 45"-wide coordinating cotton print fabric (Print A) for the side borders and quilt back

• ½ yard of another 45"-wide coordinating cotton print fabric (Print B) for the upper and lower borders

• ¼ yard of another 45"-wide coordinating cotton print fabric (Print C) for the horizontal sashing strips

• ⅝ yard of another 45"-wide coordinating cotton print fabric (Print D) for the vertical sashing strips and bias binding

• One 38" square of polyester fleece

• 1 yard of fusible transfer web

• Fabric dye, such as Starlite Dye™ by Delta, in assorted colors of your choice. *Note:* Although Starlite Dye is formulated for dark fabrics, when used on light fabrics it produces intense colors, particularly appealing to children.

• Water-soluble marker

• Matching and contrasting thread

• Several small paper plates

CUTTING

■ Prewash all fabrics.

■ Cut a 29" square from the solid fabric for the center panel.

■ Cut two 5"x37" crossgrain rectangles from Print A for the upper and lower borders and two 5"x37" rectangles from Print B for the side borders.

■ Measure in 5" from each end of the upper and lower borders along one long edge, then draw a diagonal line from each mark to the nearest adjacent corner and cut along each line (Figure 1).

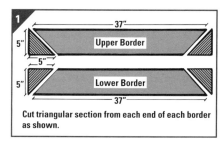

Cut triangular section from each end of each border as shown.

Repeat with the side borders.

■ Cut six 3"x11" strips from Print C for horizontal sashing strips.

■ Cut two 3"x31" strips from Print D for vertical sashing strips.

CONSTRUCTION

Note: Use ½" seam allowances throughout.

■ Right side up, divide and mark the center panel into nine squares, using the water-soluble marker, as shown in Figure 2, page 61.

■ Place the panel right side up on a large plastic-covered surface (dry cleaner bags work well).

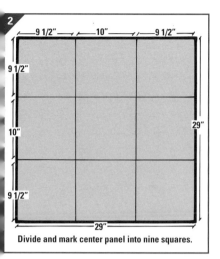

Divide and mark center panel into nine squares.

■ Pour a small amount of fabric dye onto a paper plate. Let the child place his/her hand palm side down in the dye until the palm and fingers are well coated. Have the child press his/her palm down firmly in the center of one square. *Note:* Encourage the child to simply place his/her palm on the fabric, then remove it swiftly without moving to avoid smudging.

Repeat for the remaining squares, changing dye colors (and children's hand prints) as desired. Have the child (or children) sign and date the quilt using the dye, if desired. Allow the panel to dry undisturbed overnight.

■ Heat-set the dye by placing the hand-printed panel in a warm to hot dryer for approximately 20 minutes.

■ Right sides together, stitch the border sections together, first stitching one end of each side border to opposite ends

of the upper border, then stitching the remaining side border ends to opposite ends of the lower border, ending the stitching ½" from each inside corner; press the seams open (Figure 3).

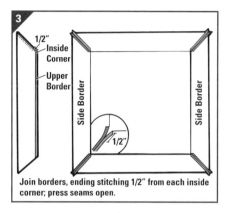

Join borders, ending stitching 1/2" from each inside corner; press seams open.

■ Right sides together, stitch the border to the center panel, breaking the stitching at each corner, to create the quilt top (Figure 4). Press the seam allowances toward the border, then press the border out flat.

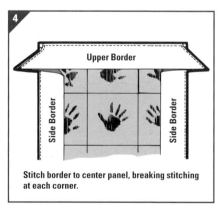

Stitch border to center panel, breaking stitching at each corner.

■ Press under ½" along each sashing strip long edge, then along each sashing strip short edge.

■ Right side up, anchor one short edge of one sashing strip to a padded pressing surface by pinning at the short edge center, then 1" from the end along each long edge. Fold the corners in to meet at the center, press to form a miter, then remove the pins; repeat at the strip's opposite end (Figure 5).

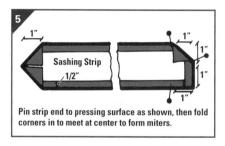

Pin strip end to pressing surface as shown, then fold corners in to meet at center to form miters.

Repeat with the remaining sashing strips.

■ Apply fusible transfer web to each sashing strip wrong side. Remove the fusible web backing paper from each strip.

■ Center one vertical sashing strip on the panel right side over each vertical marked line, so the points extend equally (approximately 1") into the upper and lower borders (Figure 6, page 62). Fuse the strips in place, following the manufacturer's instructions.

■ Center one horizontal sashing strip on the panel right side over each horizontal marked line, so the points either extend into a side border or meet an adjacent horizontal sashing strip at the center of a vertical sashing strip (Figure 7, page 62). Fuse the strips in place, following

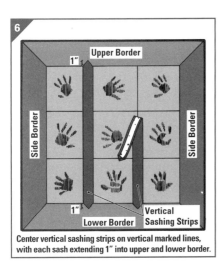

6

Upper Border

1"

Side Border

Side Border

1"

Lower Border

Vertical Sashing Strips

Center vertical sashing strips on vertical marked lines, with each sash extending 1" into upper and lower border.

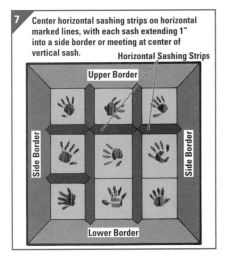

7

Center horizontal sashing strips on horizontal marked lines, with each sash extending 1" into a side border or meeting at center of vertical sash.

Horizontal Sashing Strips

Upper Border

Side Border

Side Border

Lower Border

the manufacturer's instructions.

■ Spread the remainder of Print A wrong side up on a large, flat surface. Cover the fabric with the batting, then center the quilt panel right side up on the batting. Pin the layers together at 3" to 4" intervals along the center panel outer edges, the sashing strips and the borders. Trim the batting and backing fabric approx-

imately 1" larger than the quilt top.

■ Machine baste the layers together ½" from the border outer edges, then trim the batting and backing fabric even with the quilt top.

■ Using a decorative machine stitch, such as the feather stitch, machine quilt the layers together, stitching along the center panel/border seam first (between the sashing strips), then around the vertical sashing strips' outer edges and finally around the horizontal sashing strip's outer edges (Figure 8).

■ Using the remainder of Print D, cut and piece enough 2½"-wide bias strips to create 4⅛ yards. *Note:* An 11"x 45" fabric

8

Use decorative stitch to machine quilt layers together along border/center panel seam, then around vertical sashing strips, then around horizontal sashing strips.

Border/ Center Panel Seam

Vertical Sashing Strip   Horizontal Sashing Strips

rectangle will yield enough strips to create 4⅛ yards.

■ Use the bias binding to encase the quilt raw edges (see "Applying Bias Binding" on page 83 for instructions for applying bias binding). ❏

— NO-KNOT BUTTONS —

This simple technique can make easy work of stitching buttons in place:
■ Mark the button position.
■ Thread the needle with a doubled strand of thread. *Note:* Run the thread through beeswax to help strengthen it and prevent tangles.
■ Insert the needle on the garment underside, approximately 1" from the button position, and tunnel it between the fabric layers, bringing the needle up at the button position. Take a few backstitches to lock the thread.
Note: To give sew-through buttons some "wearing ease," insert a toothpick or small crochet hook between the button and the fabric.

■ Bring the needle through the button and back down into the fabric; repeat four or five times.
■ Form the thread shank by removing the toothpick and winding the thread several times around the excess thread underneath the button.
■ Bring the needle to the garment underside and fasten with several tiny backstitches.
■ Insert the needle into the fabric and tunnel it between the layers for approximately 1". Bring the needle out on the fabric underside, then clip the beginning and ending threads close to the fabric.
Note: If the garment is single-layer or the fabric is sheer, clip the thread close to the backstitches instead of tunneling it. ❏

hairport hanger

f organization isn't one of your little gal's strong suits, entice her to keep her hair accessories corralled with the "Hairport Hanger," a multi-faceted ribbon, hairband, barrette and headband caddy that combines function with fashion. See-through pockets and serged decorative details will captivate your daughter—and remind her to put her pretty hair accessories in their place.

MATERIALS

• ⅜ yard of 45"- or 60"-wide cotton or cotton-blend fabric

• ⅜ yard of heavyweight fusible interfacing

• ⅛ yard of clear, lightweight vinyl

• Two spools of heavy decorative thread or sewing ribbon

• Two spools of all-purpose sewing thread to match fabric

• One 11¼"-long, ¼"-diameter wooden dowel

• 1½ yards of ³⁄₁₆"-wide, double-faced, picot-edge satin ribbon

• Three hook-and-loop tape circles for medium- to heavy-weight fabric

• Water-soluble marker

• Grease pencil

• Seam sealant, such as Fray Check™

• Serger

CUTTING/PREPARATION

■ Using the water-soluble marker and the cutting layout in Figure 1, draw the following rectangles onto single-thickness fabric: 9½"x 24½" for the caddy body; four 2"x 9½", one for the lower panel and three for the barrette holders; and three 2"x 5½" for the loops. Using the grease pencil, draw two 4"x 9½" pockets onto single-thickness clear vinyl. Also, draw one 9½"x 24½" rectangle on the interfacing. Cut out all of the rectangles.

Note: If desired for later use, first create patterns from tissue or pattern tracing cloth, then pin them to the fabric or tape them to the vinyl.

■ Following the manufacturer's instructions, fuse the interfacing rectangle to the caddy body wrong side; set the caddy body aside.

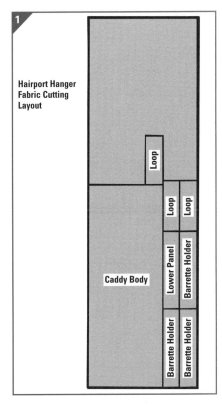

Hairport Hanger
Fabric Cutting
Layout

Loop

Loop Loop

Caddy Body Lower Panel Barrette Holder

Barrette Holder Barrette Holder

■ Using the grease pencil, mark the widthwise center on each vinyl pocket; set the pocket aside.

■ Set the serger for a balanced, wide, 3-thread stitch and a stitch length of 2 to 2½; use the all-purpose thread in the needle and the decorative thread in the loopers. Set the conventional machine for a 12-stitch-per-inch straight stitch using all-purpose thread.

CONSTRUCTION

■ Serge both long edges of each vinyl pocket, trimming ⅛"; apply seam sealant to the stitching ends and let it dry.

■ Serge, seal and trim the lower pocket panel long edges as described above for the vinyl pockets.

■ Right sides together, fold each barrette holder rectangle in half lengthwise; seam ¼" from the long raw edges on each. Turn each barrette holder right side out, press with the seam at the center back and topstitch close to each long edge (Figure 2).

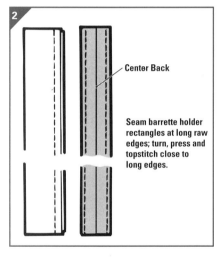

Seam barrette holder rectangles at long raw edges; turn, press and topstitch close to long edges.

Center Back

■ Stitch and topstitch the loop rectangles as described above for the barrette holder rectangles, but also seam one short end before turning and press with the seam at one long edge.

■ Position the halves of a hook-and-loop tape circle at opposite ends of each loop; stitch in place using a triangle of straight stitching (Figure 3).

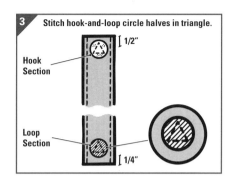

3 — Stitch hook-and-loop circle halves in triangle.

Hook Section — ⌐ 1/2"

Loop Section — ⌐ 1/4"

■ Referring to the placement guide in Figure 4 :

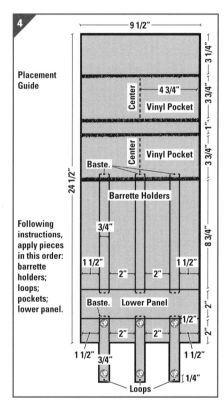

4 — Placement Guide

9 1/2"

Center — 4 3/4"
Vinyl Pocket

Center — Vinyl Pocket

Baste.

Barrette Holders

3/4"

1 1/2" — 2" — 2" — 1 1/2"

Baste. — Lower Panel

1/2"
2" — 2"

1 1/2" — 3/4" — 1 1/2"

Loops — 1/4"

24 1/2"

3 1/4" / 3 3/4" / 1" / 3 3/4" / 8 3/4" / 2" / 2"

Following instructions, apply pieces in this order: barrette holders; loops; pockets; lower panel.

• Position and baste the barrette holder ends in place.

• Position and baste one end of each loop in place.

• Position the vinyl pockets in place, being sure when positioning the lower pocket that

the barrette holder ends are covered without extending into the pocket area. Baste the pocket sides and bottom through the serging, then straight stitch along the center of each.

• Position the lower panel, covering the barrette holder and loop ends. Straight stitch across both long edges, catching the barrette holder ends in the upper edge stitching and the loop ends in the lower edge stitching.

■ Serge around all of the caddy edges, trimming ⅛"; work slowly and help the serger presser foot over thick layers by lifting the back of the foot slightly until the "lump" passes. Apply seam sealant to the stitching ends, let it dry and trim the excess chain.

■ Fold down 1" at the caddy upper edge to the caddy wrong side to form a casing; stitch close to the serged edge (Figure 5). Insert the dowel through the casing.

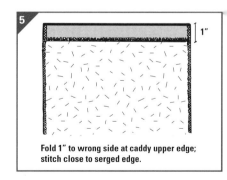

5 — 1"

Fold 1" to wrong side at caddy upper edge; stitch close to serged edge.

■ Cut an 18" length of ribbon and tie one end to each end of the dowel in a double knot. Trim the ribbon ends.

■ Cut three 6" lengths of ribbon and tie each into a bow. Tack a bow at the underside of each loop end.

■ To use the caddy, place hairbands and ribbons in the pockets, clip barrettes to the barrette holder strips and fasten the hook-and-loop tape circles on the loops to hold headbands. ❏

— EDGE IT EASY! —

Lace, one of the most elegant and feminine finishes for almost any edge, is easy to attach using the zigzag stitch on your sewing machine.

TWO-STEP APPLICATION

■ Place the lace straight edge along the seamline and stitch it in place with a fairly close, medium-width zigzag.
■ From the reverse side, trim the fabric close to the stitching.

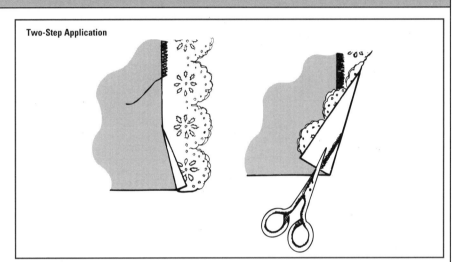

Two-Step Application

THREE-STEP APPLICATION

This technique takes the above method one step further for a more secure application.
■ Stitch as above, but use a widely spaced zigzag.
■ Fold the fabric edge back against the zigzag stitching and stitch again from the right side, using a slightly wider and denser zigzag.
■ Trim the fabric close to the stitching line. ❏

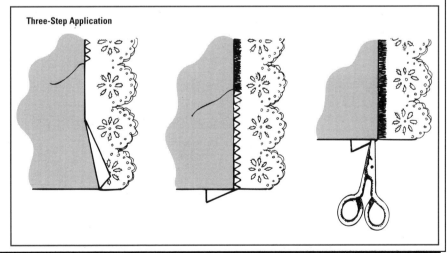

Three-Step Application

TOYS/ TIME FOR FUN

Sewing for kids can combine function and fun when the focus is on learn-and-play toys and other playtime pleasures.

Whether for the playroom, bedroom or even the bathroom, children need activity toys and accessories in colors and accents to stimulate growth and inspire ingenuity and individuality. Original toys—those not advertised on Saturday morning cartoons or celebrated as the neighborhood "toy of the week"—are often the most thought-provoking and

inspirational when it comes to creativity.

Encourage your child's imagination to wander into the wild, wild west when he or she dons the Ultrasuede® chaps and vest in "Cowboy Kudos." This simple ensemble requires no hems or edge finishing for a stitch-it-quick project, and it doubles as a darling Halloween costume.

"A" is for airplane, "B" is for balloon..."Blocks For Babes" relies on sprightly appliqués of these and other tiny wonders to teach the ABCs to inquisitive tots. The story includes

full-size patterns for simple use, and the blocks are constructed to be machine-washable so they can be used—not just admired.

"Tiny Town" also utilizes appliqués—purchased varieties or those of your own device—to create a village scene on a portable play mat. Instructions for making the mat are the focus of the story—your job (and your child's!) is to define the theme of this small town. Let your children exercise their own creativity for determining this theme, based on the toy cars, farm animals, spacecraft and other accessories they plan to use in their own little hamlet. This is a wonderful toy for on-the-go families, as it packs up into a tiny, go-anywhere bundle.

A bit of sewing savvy and a bevy of originality are all you'll need to create these time-for-fun projects sure to please parents and children alike. And you'll feel extra good knowing your children are playing with your one-of-a-kind creations that required love and thought to inspire fun and learning. ❏

Color photo of finished project on page 15

tiny town

Have you ever wished you could compact all those Gobots™ and Hotwheels™ into one small area where the kids could have fun and you could move about with the sure knowledge that you or another unwary adult would not eventually stamp out a treasured toy or sprain an ankle?

Road mat to the rescue! Easily a two- or three-hour toy for active toddlers, this miniature village gives youngsters the chance to tour the town while still in the confines of a 45"-diameter circle. And when playtime is over, cleanup is a breeze—simply gather up the mat edges, leaving all the miniature cars in place and turning the road mat into its own convenient storage bag.

ROAD MAT ROUTES

This toy is not for little boys only. Complete with shopping areas, hair salons and boutiques, a road mat village has something for little girls, too. Modern miss can buzz about on her tour of errands or park her car downtown at a prestigious high-rise and pursue her career ambitions. Little brother can use his imagination to enjoy serious business or serious fun at his chosen locations.

Busy moms need not shy away from the road mat because of the project's assumed complexity. It's designed for the very busy and the relatively inexperienced. And you don't have to follow a strict pattern or specific guidelines; your imagination and creativity are your only boundaries.

Plan your village based on who will play with the road mat and the toys they will use. Some ideas: Design a Victorian village for the little miss who loves lace and feminine frills, using eyelet, narrow ribbon and tiny floral trims; if the little man of the house loves robots and space creatures, design a space village for him, complete with a rocket ship launch pad and refueling station, relying on primary-colored ribbons and trims. Use the basic instructions below as your jumping-off point, then improvise to your heart's content.

MATERIALS

- 1¼ yards each of 45"-wide solid-colored and coordinating print fabric
- Several yards of black single-fold bias tape
- Various colors of felt
- 12⅜"-diameter grommets and grommet tool or 12¾"-diameter plastic rings
- 5 yards of ¼"-diameter cording to coordinate with fabric
- Glue stick
- Thread to match fabric and felt
- Fabric paint

CONSTRUCTION

■ Cut a 45"-diameter circle from each piece of fabric.

■ Using chalk, sketch in 3"-wide roads on the solid-colored fabric circle only, referring to the photo on page 15 for guidance and leaving a 2" margin around the fabric circle's outer edge (Figure 1, page 69).

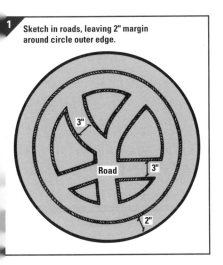

1 Sketch in roads, leaving 2" margin around circle outer edge.

3"

Road 3"

2"

■ Edgestitch the finished circle, then topstitch 1" from the edgestitching (Figure 2).

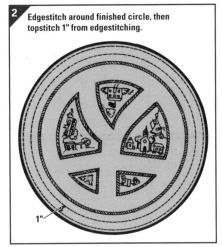

2 Edgestitch around finished circle, then topstitch 1" from edgestitching.

1"

Or, stitch plastic rings around the road mat's outer edges at approximately 12" intervals, then thread the cording through the rings and knot the ends (Figure 4).

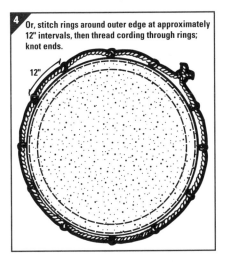

4 Or, stitch rings around outer edge at approximately 12" intervals, then thread cording through rings; knot ends.

12"

■ Edgestitch bias tape in place along the sketched lines to not only outline the roads, but create sidewalks as well, mitering the corners where necessary and turning under the raw ends.

■ From felt scraps, cut out proportionally sized structures and props. Some options include houses, shops, office buildings, trees, flowers, a park, a church, a lake—anything you want in your road mat village. Glue-baste each piece in place in the desired location, then use matching thread to edgestitch each shape in place.

■ Raw edges matching, pin the embellished and print fabric circles right sides together; stitch in a ½" seam, leaving a 5" to 6" opening for turning. Turn the circles right side out, press and slipstitch the opening closed.

■ Working from the road mat lining (print) side, install grommets at approximately 12" intervals around the road mat edge, centering each between the edgestitching and the topstitching (Figure 3). Thread the cording through the grommets, then knot the ends.

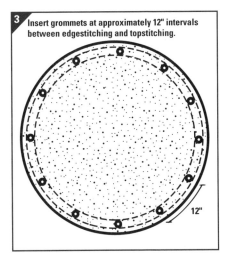

3 Insert grommets at approximately 12" intervals between edgestitching and topstitching.

12"

■ Use fabric paint, decorative machine stitching, topstitching and tiny appliqués to embellish the buildings, trees and foliage as desired. ❑

— KID-BITS —

From the Renaissance until World War I, elaborately dressed dolls were the vehicle for showing the latest fashions. After their fashion "debut," the dolls became children's toys. Paper dolls were also used to translate fashion from one area of the world to another.

blocks for babes

Oh baby! These appliquéd ABC soft blocks will be a favorite learning toy for baby, their sturdy construction making them a usable accent for the playroom or nursery. Using bits and pieces of bright primary and pastel fabric scraps and a little ingenuity, you can stitch them in a jiffy. For variety, consider enclosing a squeaker or jingle bell inside one of the blocks to tickle the fancy of even the tiniest tot. The appliqués represent letters of the alphabet—A is for airplane, B is for balloon, etc.—but these tiny extras will make great embellishments on bibs, clothing and more.

MATERIALS

- ⅓ yard of white double-faced quilted cotton fabric
- Assorted scraps of primary and pastel fabrics in solids, mini-prints and mini-dots
- ⅓ yard of ⅛"-wide green mini-dot satin ribbon
- 6" of ⅛"-wide red mini-dot grosgrain fabric
- Fusible transfer web
- One bag of polyfill stuffing
- Matching and contrasting threads
- Shiny fabric paints, such as Scribbles® from Duncan Crafts, in several colors
- Fine-line sable paintbrush
- Air-soluble marker

CONSTRUCTION

■ Prewash all fabrics and press as necessary.

■ From the quilted fabric, cut 18 4" squares (six for each block).

■ Trace the full-size appliqué patterns in Figure 1 (pages 71, 72 and 73) and transfer each piece to the fusible web wrong side (paper side). *Note:* The letter appliqués are reversed but will result in the correct perspective when appliquéd.

■ Choose the fabric scraps to create your appliqués, using the photo on page 14 as a guide, if desired, or using your own creativity to choose appropriate fabrics. Fuse the traced-upon fusible transfer web to the selected fabrics, following the manufacturer's instructions, then cut out each appliqué piece. Remove the paper back from each appliqué piece.

■ For the "A" block:

- Center and fuse the uppercase A, lowercase A, anchor and alligator appliqués to the right side of four separate quilted squares, positioning the alligator at a diagonal.

- Center and fuse the apple appliqué components in place on one quilted square right side in the following order: stem, apple, leaf.

- Center and fuse the airplane appliqué components in place diagonally on one quilted square right side, following the placement guidelines on the pattern to fuse the window, wing and tail in place.

■ For the B block:

- Center and fuse the uppercase B and lowercase B appliqués in place on the right side of two separate quilted squares.

- Fuse the balloon appliqué in place on one quilted square right side slightly off-center toward one upper corner.

- Center and fuse the butterfly appliqué components (wings, then body) in place on one quilted square right side.

- Center and fuse the bear appliqué components in place diagonally on one quilted square right side, in the following order: collar, head, snout.

- Center and fuse the boat appliqué components in place diagonally on one quilted square right side.

■ For the C block:

- Center and fuse the uppercase C, lowercase C and carrots appliqués on the right side of three separate quilted squares.

- Center and fuse the chick appliqué components (beak, then chick) in place on one quilted square right side.

- Center and fuse the candy appliqué components in place

diagonally on one quilted square right side, following the placement guidelines to fuse the stripes in place.

- Center and fuse the clown appliqué components in place diagonally on one quilted square right side in the following order: collar, face, nose, hair, hat and hat ball.

Leaf

Stem

Apple

Boat

Flag

Sail   Sail

Body

Balloon

Butterfly

Body

Bear

Head

Snout

Collar

Wings

Candy   Stripes

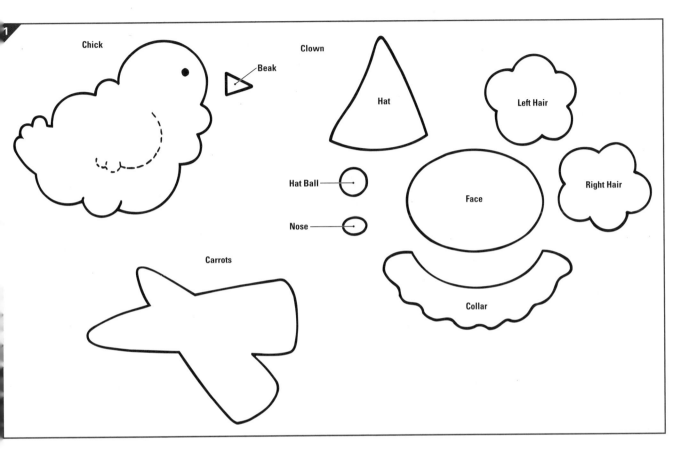

Chick

Beak

Clown

Hat

Left Hair

Hat Ball

Nose

Face

Right Hair

Carrots

Collar

■ Using matching or contrasting thread and a medium-width, zigzag satin stitch, appliqué each piece in place (see "Super Satin Stitching" on page 76 for tips on successful satin stitching).

■ Add the following stitched and fabric painted accents:

• Fabric paint the alligator appliqué's facial features in your choice of colors, then make a tiny bow from the red mini-dot grosgrain ribbon and tack it in place to the chin area (Figure 2).

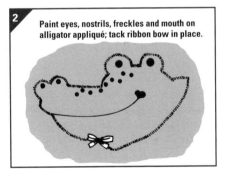

2 Paint eyes, nostrils, freckles and mouth on alligator appliqué; tack ribbon bow in place.

• Continue the satin stitching into the apple appliqué at the apple upper edge as indicated on the pattern, then use contrasting thread to add a satin stitched "worm hole," according to the pattern.

• Add a satin stitched propeller to the nose of the airplane appliqué (Figure 3).

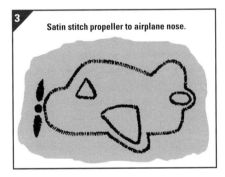

3 Satin stitch propeller to airplane nose.

• Using contrasting thread and two rows of straight stitching (one on top of the other), add a balloon string to the balloon appliqué; fabric paint an accent mark on the balloon Figure 4.

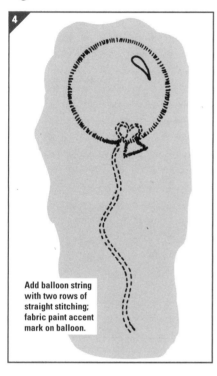

Add balloon string with two rows of straight stitching; fabric paint accent mark on balloon.

• Satin stitch the antennae on the butterfly appliqué using thread to match the butterfly body (Figure 5).

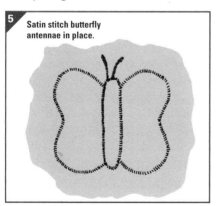

Satin stitch butterfly antennae in place.

• Straight stitch across the base of each ear on the bear appliqué, then fabric paint the inner ears, cheeks, eyes, eyebrows, nose and mouth in place (Figure 6).

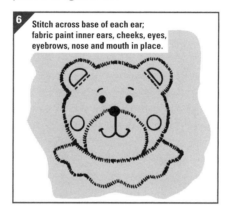

Stitch across base of each ear; fabric paint inner ears, cheeks, eyes, eyebrows, nose and mouth in place.

• Satin stitch two scalloped rows of water beneath the boat appliqué as shown in Figure 7.

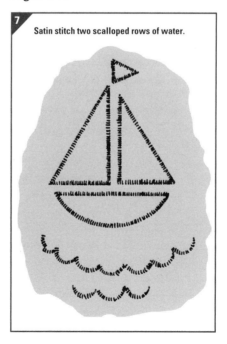

Satin stitch two scalloped rows of water.

• Using matching thread, add straight stitch detailing on the carrots, then, using the green satin mini-dot ribbon, tack three ribbon loops to each carrot top to indicate "greens" (Figure 8).

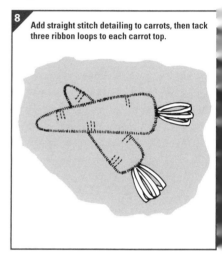

Add straight stitch detailing to carrots, then tack three ribbon loops to each carrot top.

• Using matching thread, satin stitch the wing detail on the chick appliqué, according to the guidelines on the pattern, then, using contrasting thread, satin stitch the legs, feet and eye in place (Figure 9).

Satin stitch wing detail, plus feet and eye.

• Fabric paint eyes, eyebrows, cheeks, mouth and chin in place on the clown appliqué (Figure 10).

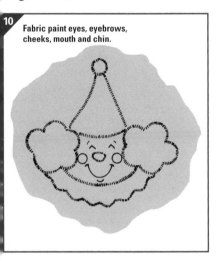

10 Fabric paint eyes, eyebrows, cheeks, mouth and chin.

■ Allow all the fabric paint to dry completely.

■ Using the air-soluble marker, make a dot on each square wrong side ¼" from each corner.

■ Arrange six squares for each block (A block: A, a, anchor, alligator, apple, airplane); (B block: B, b, balloon, butterfly, bear, boat); (C block: C, c, carrots, chick, candy, clown) and number each square as shown in Figure 11. Be sure all appliqués are positioned in the same direction for each set.

■ Right sides together and using ¼" seam allowances, stitch each square together from dot to dot (do *not* stitch to the end of each square): Stitch down the vertical four-square row (squares 1, 2, 3 and 4), then stitch square 5 to

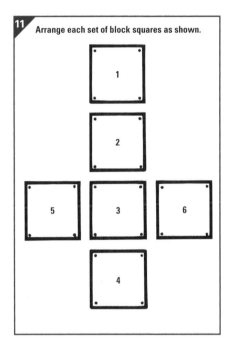

11 Arrange each set of block squares as shown.

square 3 and square 6 to square 3, forming a three-square horizontal row (squares 5, 3 and 6) (Figure 12).

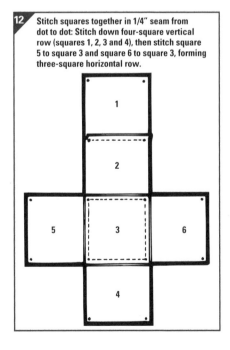

12 Stitch squares together in 1/4" seam from dot to dot: Stitch down four-square vertical row (squares 1, 2, 3 and 4), then stitch square 5 to square 3 and square 6 to square 3, forming three-square horizontal row.

■ Fold up the squares so the right-angle edges of the following squares meet: 2 and 5; 2 and 6; 4 and 5; and 4 and 6 (Figure 13); pin.

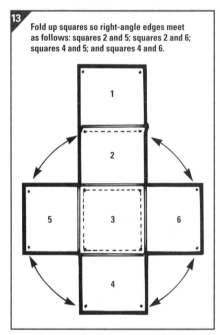

13 Fold up squares so right-angle edges meet as follows: squares 2 and 5; squares 2 and 6; squares 4 and 5; and squares 4 and 6.

■ Right sides together and using a ¼" seam allowance, stitch each pinned edge together from dot to dot to form the block corners. Right sides together, stitch the edge of square 5 to square 1 and square 6 to square 1. *Note:* All except one edge (squares 1 and 4) should now be stitched (Figure 14, page 76).

— KID·BITS —

Coral has been used for children's rattles and beads for centuries because it's believed to bring good luck.

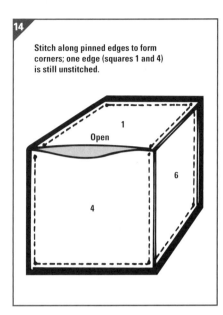

14

Stitch along pinned edges to form corners; one edge (squares 1 and 4) is still unstitched.

■ Turn the block right side out. Press under ¼" along the raw edges of squares 1 and 4, stuff the block firmly with fiberfill and blind stitch this edge closed (Figure 15).

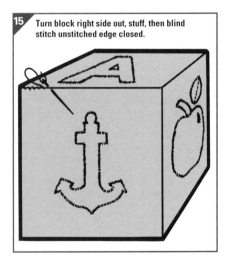

15

Turn block right side out, stuff, then blind stitch unstitched edge closed.

— SUPER SATIN STITCHING —

■ To satin stitch the sharp points in appliquéd designs, stitch to each corner and stop with the needle in the fabric at the *outer* position. Raise the presser foot and continue stitching, overlapping the stitching slightly at the corner area (Figure 1).

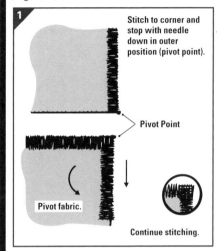

1

Stitch to corner and stop with needle down in outer position (pivot point).

Pivot Point

Pivot fabric.

Continue stitching.

■ To satin stitch outer curves, begin with the needle in the fabric on the curve *inside*:

• Move the flywheel by hand, taking one stitch to the outside and back to the inside, returning the needle to the *original hole* on the curve inside.

Raise the presser foot and *pivot the fabric slightly*; lower the presser foot, take another stitch and return the needle to the *original hole*.

Repeat.

• For the next stitch, lift the needle, push the fabric back a little and insert the needle on the inside curve just a fraction of an inch from the previous inside needle hole.

• Repeat the above steps until you've completed the curve (Figure 2).

2

Stitch three times in each inside curve hole, pivoting slightly at outside curve.

Move fabric slightly and repeat.

■ To satin stitch a scallop point, mark the inner point of the scallop and stitch to the mark as you would stitch a sharp point or corner; raise the presser foot and pivot the fabric as needed; lower the presser foot and continue stitching, overlapping the stitching slightly at the scallop point area (Figure 3).

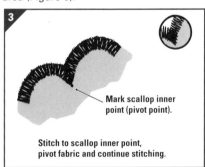

3

Mark scallop inner point (pivot point).

Stitch to scallop inner point, pivot fabric and continue stitching.

for photo finished projects on page 14

bath time splash

Make taking a bath extra special for your favorite cherub with this cozy, after-bath wrap-up and matching bath mitt. For the perfect gift, add some baby shampoo, powder, mild soap and a teddy bear water toy, then wrap up the entire ensemble. Baby will find bath time oh-sew-"bearable."

MATERIALS

• 1⅝ yards of 45"-wide white velour terry cloth

• 6 yards of red, extra-wide, double-fold bias tape

• One 4½"x 9" rectangle of a colorful 100-percent cotton calico print fabric

• One 7"x10" rectangle of brown synthetic suede, such as Ultrasuede® or Facile®

• Small scraps of synthetic suede, such as Ultrasuede® or Facile® in the following colors: red, medium pink and light pink

• ⅓ yard of ⅛"-wide, double-faced red satin ribbon

• ½ yard of fusible transfer web

• Black, white and red embroidery floss

• Matching thread

• Air- or water-soluble marker

CUTTING

■ Preshrink the terry cloth and calico fabric. *Note:* Serge-finish the terry cloth raw edges to prevent excess raveling before preshrinking, if desired.

■ From the terry cloth, cut a 36" square for the wrap, rounding each corner.

■ Apply fusible transfer web to the wrong side of each piece of synthetic suede and the calico fabric, following the manufacturer's instructions.

■ Trace the full-sized patterns in Figure 1 and cut the following: two hearts from red synthetic suede; two snouts from pale pink synthetic suede; and eight paw pads and four inner ears from medium pink synthetic suede.

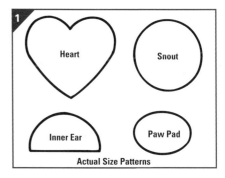

1
Heart Snout
Inner Ear Paw Pad
Actual Size Patterns

■ Enlarge the patterns in Figure 2, page 78, and cut the following: two rompers from the calico fabric; two bears from the brown synthetic suede; and one hood and two mitts from the terry cloth. Round the hood's right angle corner to match the wrap corners.

APPLIQUÉING

■ Remove the transfer web paper backing and fuse the inner ears, snout and paw pads to each bear right side and a heart to each romper right side bib area as shown in Figure 3, page 78.

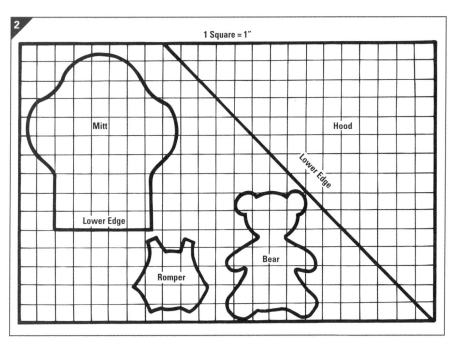

2

1 Square = 1"

Mitt

Hood

Lower Edge

Lower Edge

Romper

Bear

5

Romper

Fuse romper to each bear right side.

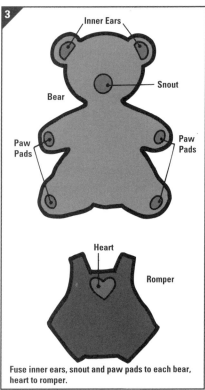

3

Inner Ears

Bear

Snout

Paw Pads

Paw Pads

Heart

Romper

Fuse inner ears, snout and paw pads to each bear, heart to romper.

■ Use three strands of white embroidery floss to make a cluster of four French knots for each bear eye; use three strands of black embroidery floss to satin stitch a nose on the each snout; and use three strands of red embroidery floss to satin stitch a mouth on each snout (Figure 4).

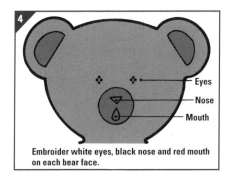

4

Eyes

Nose

Mouth

Embroider white eyes, black nose and red mouth on each bear face.

■ Fuse one romper to each bear right side, matching all outer edges (Figure 5); trim uneven edges as necessary.

■ Center a bear on one mitt right side, the other bear on the hood right side 3" from the lower edge as shown in Figure 6; remove the transfer web paper backing and fuse each in place.

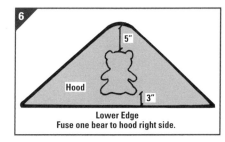

6

5"

Hood

3"

Lower Edge
Fuse one bear to hood right side.

■ Using matching thread, machine satin stitch each bear in place around the outer edges and across the neck area between the arm upper edges to differentiate between the head and the body.

■ Using matching thread, machine satin stitch around each romper and across each "waistline," then from this line to the romper lower edge to indicate a center front seam (Figure 7).

Satin stitch around romper edges, then across romper, creating a "waistline" and center front seam.

■ To secure the inner ears, snout, paw pads and heart permanently on each bear: Using matching thread, machine blind stitch over the raw edges of each piece (Figure 8).

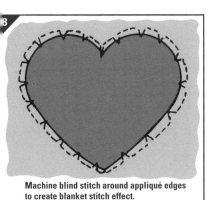

Machine blind stitch around appliqué edges to create blanket stitch effect.

CONSTRUCTION

■ Encase the hood and mitt lower edges with bias tape, creating a decorative effect, if desired, by using white thread and the machine blind hem stitching to apply the bias tape (Figure 9).

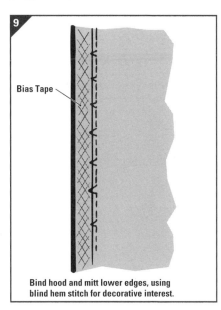

Bind hood and mitt lower edges, using blind hem stitch for decorative interest.

■ *Wrong* sides together and raw edges matching, baste the mitts together ¼" from the unbound edges.

■ *Wrong* sides together and raw edges matching, place the hood against the wrap, matching the hood curved corner to one wrap corner; baste the outer edges together ¼" from the edge (Figure 10).

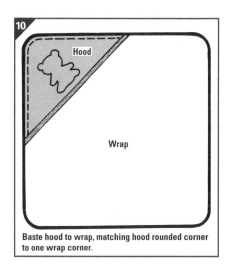

Baste hood to wrap, matching hood rounded corner to one wrap corner.

■ Encase all remaining raw edges with bias tape, turning the bias tape raw ends under at the joining and mitt lower edges.

■ Cut the ribbon into two 6"-long pieces and tie each into a tiny bow; tack one bow to each bear neckline.

❑

— KID-BITS —

Until the late 1920s, shorts were worn only by small boys and tropical dwellers. Sunbathing and sports brought them into adult fashion at this time.

cowboy kudos

Your aspiring western hero will love dressing up in his or her authentic western gear for riding the range during playtime. Make the outfit from synthetic suede, such as Ultrasuede®, for a durable ensemble. Or, use washable felt if durability is not important or you want to make a minimal investment.

Dad can be involved in this project, too. Ask him to help by attaching silver nailheads to the fringed vest and chaps. Don't forget an outlaw's bandanna and cowboy hat to complete the look, which is sure to become a make-believe favorite for months to come.

Note: The following materials and patterns will yield an ensemble to fit children sized 4 to 6; adapt as necessary to fit a larger or smaller child.

MATERIALS

- ¾ yard of 45"-wide synthetic suede, such as Ultrasuede, or washable felt
- Approximately 125 ⁷⁄₁₆"-diameter nailheads (also called round nickel spots)
- Gluestick
- Pattern tracing cloth
- Matching thread
- Water-soluble marker
- Awl
- Small hammer

CUTTING

■ Enlarge the patterns in Figure 1.

■ From synthetic suede or felt cut the following, using a "with nap" layout to avoid shading variations:

- One vest back.
- Two vest fronts, two chaps pieces and two yokes/belt loop extensions, reversing one of each to cut a left and right side.
- Two 1½"x10½" strips for the upper leg straps.
- Two 1½"x9" strips for the lower leg straps.

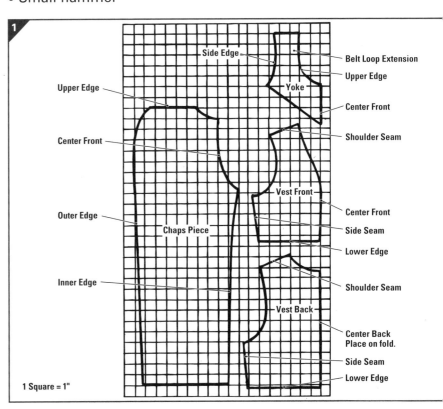

1 Square = 1"

- Two 2"x 2¾" rectangles for the vest fringed flaps.
- Two ¼"x10" strips for the chaps ties.

CONSTRUCTION

■ Position one flap rectangle on each vest front 1" from the center front and 2½" from the lower edge, as shown in Figure 2.

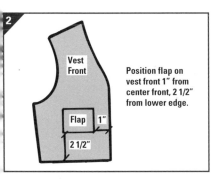

Vest Front

Flap 1"

2 1/2"

Position flap on vest front 1" from center front, 2 1/2" from lower edge.

■ Edgestitch each flap in place along the upper edge only. Working from the lower edge up, make 1¼"-deep slashes spaced ³⁄₁₆" apart on each flap to create the fringe (Figure 3).

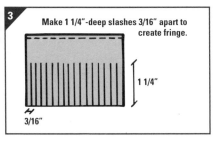

Make 1 1/4"-deep slashes 3/16" apart to create fringe.

1 1/4"

3/16"

■ Working with the pieces right sides up, overlap the vest fronts over the vest back at the shoulder seam edges, positioning each front shoulder edge at its respective back shoulder ⅝" stitching line; glue-baste in place. Allow the glue to dry, then edgestitch each in place along the vest front shoulder raw edges; trim each vest back shoulder seam allowance to ⅛" (Figure 4).

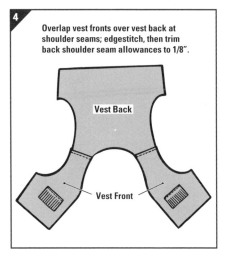

Overlap vest fronts over vest back at shoulder seams; edgestitch, then trim back shoulder seam allowances to 1/8".

Vest Back

Vest Front

■ Apply four or five nailheads evenly spaced across each flap above the fringe and evenly spaced across each vest front shoulder seam in front of the edgestitching (Figure 5), following the manufacturer's instructions. *Note:* Nailheads should pierce only *one* layer of suede at each location.

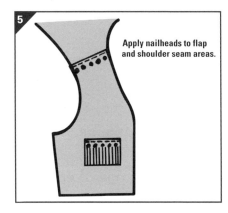

Apply nailheads to flap and shoulder seam areas.

■ Overlap the vest fronts over the vest back at the side seam edges, positioning each front side edge at its respective back side edge ⅝" stitching line; glue-baste in place. Allow the glue to dry, then edgestitch in place along the vest front side edges; trim each vest back side seam allowance to ⅛".

■ Fringe the vest front lower edge by making 2"-deep slashes ³⁄₁₆" apart beginning ½" from each center front and proceeding to each side seam.

■ Fringe the outer edge of each chaps piece by making 2"-deep slashes ³⁄₁₆" apart along each chaps piece length, beginning at the chaps lower edge.

■ Knot one end of each chaps tie.

■ With each piece right side up, position the unknotted end of one chaps tie on each chaps piece, then stitch in place in a reinforced rectangle pattern, as shown in Figure 6.

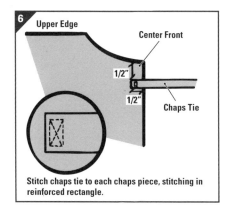

Upper Edge

Center Front

1/2"

1/2"

Chaps Tie

Stitch chaps tie to each chaps piece, stitching in reinforced rectangle.

■ With each piece right side up, position one yoke on each

chaps piece, matching the upper and center front raw edges (Figure 7); glue-baste in place. Allow the glue to dry, then edgestitch along the chaps upper edge to secure the yoke.

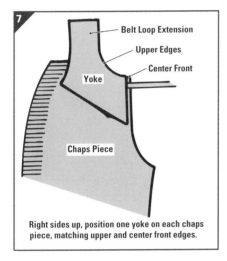

Right sides up, position one yoke on each chaps piece, matching upper and center front edges.

■ Fold the belt loop extension to the chaps wrong side, with the upper raw edges matching; edgestitch in place just above the chaps upper edge (Figure 8).

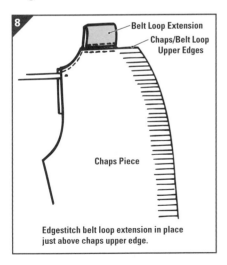

Edgestitch belt loop extension in place just above chaps upper edge.

■ Working from the center front to the side edge, fringe each yoke, making the slashes ³⁄₁₆" apart and gradually decreasing the length of each slash as you approach each side edge (Figure 9).

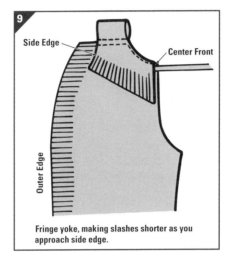

Fringe yoke, making slashes shorter as you approach side edge.

■ With each piece wrong side up, position two leg straps on each chaps piece outer edge area 1" from the fringe, positioning the upper leg strap 2" below the crotch line, the lower leg strap 3" above the lower edge (Figure 10). Glue-baste, then edgestitch each leg strap end in place along its 1½" edge.

■ Position and apply nailheads evenly spaced along each chaps piece outer edge ½" from the fringe, using approximately 40 nailheads for the length of each chaps piece.

■ Glue-baste, then edgestitch, the unstitched end of each leg strap in place ½" from the chaps inner edge, then apply

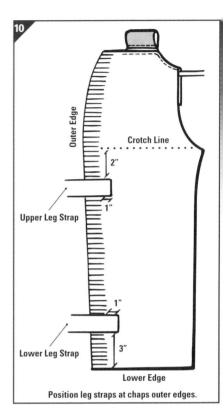

Position leg straps at chaps outer edges.

two nailheads at this stitching as shown in Figure 11.

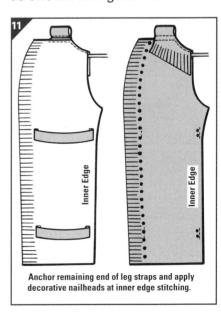

Anchor remaining end of leg straps and apply decorative nailheads at inner edge stitching.

Dress your little cowpoke in the new duds over a pair of blue jeans and a flannel or chambray shirt as follows: Simply slip his or her legs through the chaps leg straps and thread a belt through the jeans and chaps belt loops; add the vest, a hat and a bandanna and let him "saddle up!" ❑

— APPLYING BIAS BINDING —

Binding the edges of children's apparel and accessories renders a distinct edge and very finished look. Whether you purchase binding or create your own bias tape from coordinating fabric (see "Bias Tape Made Easy" on page 115), applying this edge finish takes just a bit of practice and patience. Simply follow these tips:

Note: The following guidelines refer to the *garment* edge for instructional purposes; however, bias binding can be applied as an edge finish to other projects as well.

STRAIGHT OR CURVED EDGE

■ If you're using binding you've created yourself, press under one-quarter of the binding width along one long edge.
■ Open out one fold of purchased bias tape or work along the unfolded edge of custom-made bias.
■ Raw edges even and right sides together, pin the binding to the garment edge, turning under the bias ends flush with the garment edge (Figure 1).

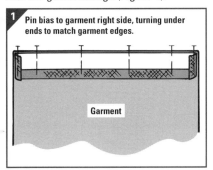

1 Pin bias to garment right side, turning under ends to match garment edges.

Garment

Note: When applying bias to an inside curve, such as a neckline edge, gently stretch the bias as it's being applied so the finished application will hug the curve. When applying bias to an outside curve, such as a Peter Pan collar, gently ease the bias around the curve to avoid a pulled look when the application is complete.

■ Stitch, using the finished binding width as your seam width. Press the seam toward the binding.
■ Turn the bias folded edge to the garment wrong side, encasing the raw edges and concealing the seam; press, then slipstitch close to the fold (Figure 2).

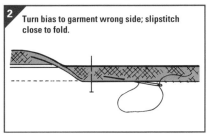

2 Turn bias to garment wrong side; slipstitch close to fold.

Note: To apply bias tape exclusively by machine, follow the instructions given above, except begin by placing the bias on the garment wrong side, then machine edgestitch the bias in place from the garment right side (Figure 3).

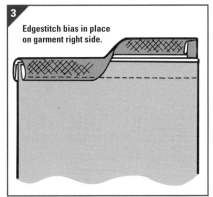

3 Edgestitch bias in place on garment right side.

MITERED OUTSIDE CORNERS

■ Stitch the bias up to the seamline crossing at the corner (Figure 4).
■ Fold the bias strip up at a diagonal, then across, with the second fold even

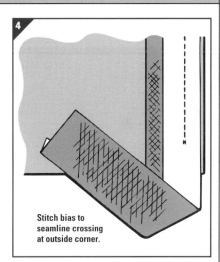

4

Stitch bias to seamline crossing at outside corner.

with the garment crosswise edge and begin stitching again exactly at the bias corner seamline (Figure 5). Continue stitching, mitering any subsequent corners in the same manner.

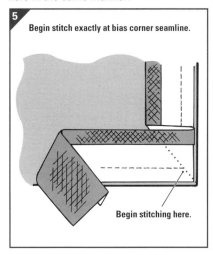

5 Begin stitch exactly at bias corner seamline.

Begin stitching here.

Continued on next page.

■ Fold the binding over the garment raw edges, carefully forming a neat miter on the garment right side (Figure 6).

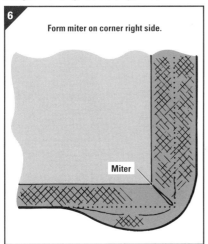

Form miter on corner right side.

Miter

■ Form a miter on the garment wrong side; pin. Slipstitch the binding final fold in place, catching the corner miter as well (Figure 7).

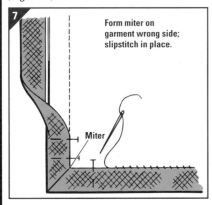

Form miter on garment wrong side; slipstitch in place.

Miter

■ Press the entire binding to set it.

MITERED INSIDE CORNERS

■ Reinforce the garment's inner corner seamline with small stitches, stitching 1" on either side of the corner. Clip into the corner, being careful not to cut the threads (Figure 8).

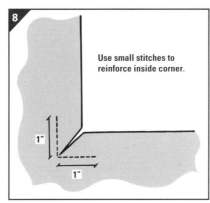

Use small stitches to reinforce inside corner.

1"

1"

■ Spread the slashed corner until the garment raw edge lies flat.

■ Stitch the binding in place along the seamline, stitching from the garment wrong side, being careful not to stitch a pleat in the garment fabric at the inside corner (Figure 9). Continue stitching, mitering any subsequent corners in the same manner.

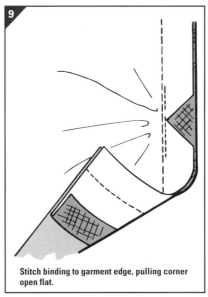

Stitch binding to garment edge, pulling corner open flat.

■ Carefully fold the binding to form a miter on the garment right side

(Figure 10). *Note:* The miter fold lies between the clipped edges.

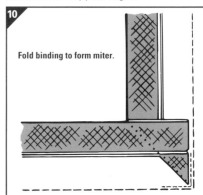

Fold binding to form miter.

■ Fold the binding over the raw edges, forming a miter on the garment wrong side; pin. Slipstitch the binding final fold in place, catching the corner miter as well (Figure 11).

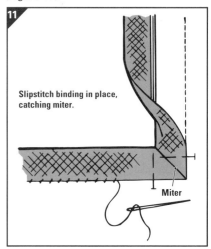

Slipstitch binding in place, catching miter.

Miter

■ Press the entire binding to set it. ❑

LITTLE TOUCHES

Perhaps anyone who sews has finished an outfit only to find that something was missing. The look was not complete, although you had followed a carefully laid sewing plan to a T. Enter, accessories. These small-but-mighty additions can truly transform the ordinary into the extraordinary. And their impact on childrenswear is no exception. In fact, children—even little ones—are captivated by any little extra that complements their clothing, which is why we see such a boom-ing accessory business in ready-to-wear. This influence is also evident in an abundance of children's ready-made clothing, replete with pockets aplenty, fancy appliqués, pert patches—anything to capture a child's attention and make the clothes as fun as they are functional.

This chapter helps you accessorize your kids from head to toe—literally. And although we offer you fabric and trim suggestions, you'll want to choose these items based on the outfits with which the accessories will be worn. Be creative with color and patterning choices, and if your child is old enough, allow him or her to assist in the selections. This not only ensures the child will use the precious extras, but it encourages the learned art of coordinating ensembles (clothing or otherwise), a talent many an adult has even yet to master.

If time is of the essence, as in most households today, consider just sewing accessories to complement ready-to-wear clothing. Even though this is a shortcut approach, it will keep you in the swing of sewing and add style to your child's wardrobe—

plus a sense of quality and prestige.

Baby headbands ("Banded Beauty") and a bevy of infant bibs ("Drool-Cool Bibs") even get new moms into the accessory-thinking mode. What a fun way to make baby's first impression—with a tiny "wardrobe" of simple-to-make headbands and unique bibs.

Older girls will love the pouf socks in "Fancy Feet," their unusual design simply an addition to ready-made crew socks. The beauty of these is you can make a pair to match every outfit you sew your little darling, using left-over scraps—and about 10 minutes!

Grade-school-aged girls and boys will love "Bitty Book Bag," a scaled-down version of an adult-sized backpack, but in exciting colors and fabrics to suit any little school-goer.

Accessorize! It's one of the most fulfilling aspects of kids' wardrobing. The main ingredient to its success is applying your originality to already-finished ensembles—something you and your little one can enjoy together.

color photo
finished project
on page 17

fancy feet

Do you take stock in your little one's socks? When you sew her a new outfit, do you long to go beyond the hemline with design ideas to neaten her tiny feet? Now you can complete any ensemble—dressy, casual or otherwise—by fashioning matching pouf socks. These trendy creations will dress up her legs in a style her friends will adore—and she'll never again be relegated to wearing the boring, basic crew and knee socks of yesteryear.

DESIGN OPTIONS

Keep the remnants from the special outfits you've created for her—that's all you'll need to polish off each look with a pair of pouf socks.

Or, help little miss sock it to her favorite holidays, using heart-print fabric to make Valentine's Day socks, orange and black fabrics for Halloween antics and red, white and blue prints and solids for celebrating the Fourth of July.

An imagination is all you need to make the most of this unique salute to the foot! Create the pouf socks, then embellish at your discretion, using lace or other trims, if desired. The following instructions are for creating one pair of single-pouf Toddler's size 4 to 6½ socks.

MATERIALS

• One pair of child's ready-made crew socks. *Note:* For the best results, use 80-percent cotton/20-percent nylon socks.

• Two 1½"x10" fabric strips to coordinate or contrast with the socks

• Matching thread

• Water-soluble marker

CONSTRUCTION

■ Measure and mark 1½" from each sock upper edge; cut along this marking (Figure 1).

■ Right sides together, fold one fabric strip in half crosswise, with the short edges matching. Stitch in a ⅝" seam to create a circle; press the seam open.

Repeat with the other fabric strip.

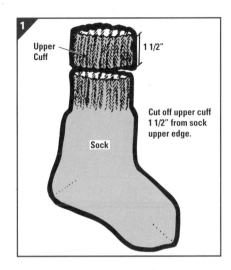

Cut off upper cuff 1 1/2" from sock upper edge.

■ Right sides together, pin one raw edge of one fabric circle to the raw edge of one upper cuff; stitch in place in a ¼" seam, stretching the upper cuff to fit the fabric (Figure 2).

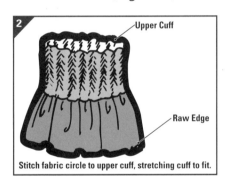

Stitch fabric circle to upper cuff, stretching cuff to fit.

Stitch again with your machine's lockstitch for reinforcement. Or, use your serger's 3-thread overlock stitch in place of the above two steps.

Repeat with the remaining upper cuff and fabric circle.

■ Right sides together, slip one upper cuff/fabric circle over one sock, matching the sock raw edge and the fabric circle raw edge; stitch in a ¼" seam, stretching the sock to fit the fabric (Figure 3).

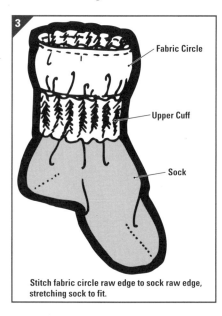

Stitch fabric circle raw edge to sock raw edge, stretching sock to fit.

Stitch again with your machine's lockstitch for reinforcement. Or, use your serger's 3-thread overlock stitch in place of the above two steps.

Repeat with the remaining upper cuff/fabric circle and sock.

■ Flip each cuff up to expose the pouf fabric (Figure 4).

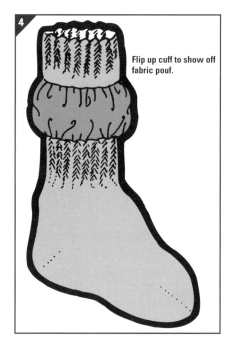

Flip up cuff to show off fabric pouf.

VARIATIONS

■ Use 3"x10" fabric strips to create more substantial poufs (refer to the photo on page 17).

■ Add lace or another trim along the cuff upper edge to complement the pouf (refer to the photo on page 17).

■ Create a double pouf on each sock (refer to the photo on page 17): Use two 1½"x10" fabric strips, then cut two 1"-wide upper cuffs on which to sew the strips as instructed under "Construction" above.   ❏

— CYCLING SAFETY —

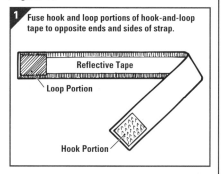

This quick-to-make sports strap is a must for kids (and adults!) who love spur-of-the-moment biking. To keep the leg of pants and sweats in their place, to keep the pants free of grease and interference with a bicycle's inner workings and to act as a night time reflector, this strap could be a life-saver—in more ways than one.

For each strap you'll need: 1"-wide grosgrain ribbon (to determine the necessary length, measure comfortably around your child's ankle over his or her pants and socks, then add 3"); ½"-wide reflective iron-on tape in the same amount as the ribbon; 1¾" of ¾"-wide iron-on hook-and-loop tape, such as Velcro®; and glue stick.

■ Fold under 1½" on each end of the ribbon, folding one end to the ribbon right side, the other end to the ribbon wrong side; glue-baste in place to create the strap.

■ Fuse the reflective tape to the strap right side.

■ Fuse the hook portion of the hook-and-loop tape on the strap *wrong* side on top of the strap's 1½" turned-back area; fuse the loop portion of the hook-and-loop tape on the strap *right* side on top of the strap's remaining 1½" turned-back area (Figure 1).

Fuse hook and loop portions of hook-and-loop tape to opposite ends and sides of strap.

Reflective Tape

Loop Portion

Hook Portion

❏

or photo nished projects on page 16

drool-cool bibs

Looking for a shower or baby gift to make that's fast, fun and cute as the dickens? This bevy of bibs will fit the bill. Search through your scrap box for most of the materials, and if you're unable to find terry cloth for "Party Perfect" and "Gerry Giraffe," simply use inexpensive bath towels. A word to the wise: Use cotton or stain-repellent fabrics for easy care and be sure to preshrink all elements before cutting and sewing.

MR. IRRESISTIBLE

Your little guy will be the hit of the high-chair jet set when you spice up his special-occasion attire with this tuxedo bib, sporting a tuxedo-front shirt, bow tie and cummerbund. Due to the combination of colors and fabrics, dry cleaning is recommended; however, other washable fabrics could be substituted—but be sure to pretreat.

MATERIALS

- 15"x20" rectangle of black cotton velveteen
- 8"x10½" and 6"x10½" rectangles of white cotton fabric
- 12"x18" rectangle of red and black plaid fabric
- 12"x18" rectangle of firmly woven black cotton fabric
- 2½"x13" rectangle of white rib knit
- 2 yards of extra-wide, black, double-fold bias tape
- Three ½"-diameter black buttons
- Water-soluble marker
- Pattern tracing cloth

CONSTRUCTION

Note: Use ½" seam allowances unless otherwise indicated.

■ Enlarge the patterns in Figure 1 and cut two bib side fronts and one bib back from the velveteen. From the plaid fabric, cut two 3½"x6" rectangles and two 3½"x5" rectan-

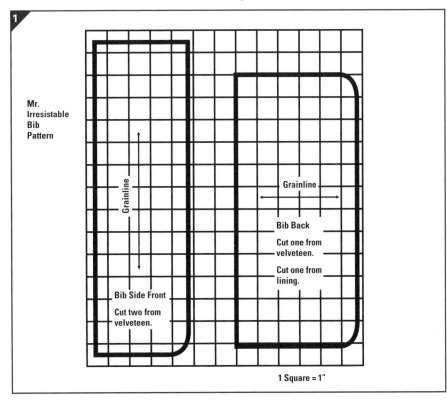

Mr. Irresistable Bib Pattern

Grainline

Grainline

Bib Back
Cut one from velveteen.
Cut one from lining.

Bib Side Front
Cut two from velveteen.

1 Square = 1"

gles, one of each on the bias, one of each on the straight grain, for the cummerbund and bow tie, respectively.

■ Wrong sides together, stitch the cummerbund rectangles together ¼" from the raw edges.

■ At each short end of the 8"x10½" white cotton rectangle (shirt front), snip-mark 1⅝" and 2½" from the long edges for the pleats (Figure 2). Make the pleats with the folds toward the long edges, then press and stitch across the short ends (Figure 3).

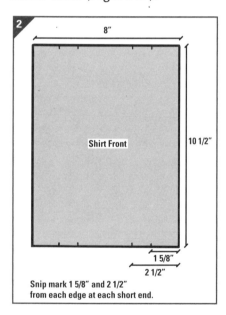

8"

Shirt Front

10 1/2"

1 5/8"

2 1/2"

Snip mark 1 5/8" and 2 1/2" from each edge at each short end.

■ Wrong sides together, stitch the 6"x10½" white cotton rectangle (shirt lining) to the pleated shirt front, then stitch the cummerbund to one short end, with the cummerbund's bias

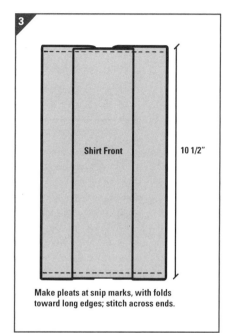

Shirt Front

10 1/2"

Make pleats at snip marks, with folds toward long edges; stitch across ends.

side against the shirt front right side (Figure 4). Press the seam toward the cummerbund.

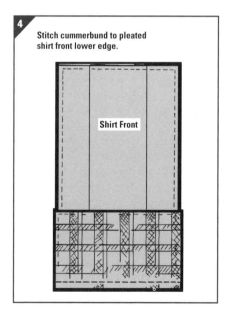

Stitch cummerbund to pleated shirt front lower edge.

Shirt Front

■ Right sides together, stitch the bib side fronts to the long edges of the shirt front/cummerbund. Trim the velveteen seam allowance to ¼". Press the seams toward the side front and topstitch ¼" from the seamlines through all thicknesses (Figure 5, page 91).

■ Right sides together, stitch the bib back to the bib front along the bib front upper edge. Trim, press and topstitch the seam as for the side front seams above.

5

Stitch side fronts to shirt front/cummerbund, press seams toward side fronts, then topstitch 1/4" from seamlines.

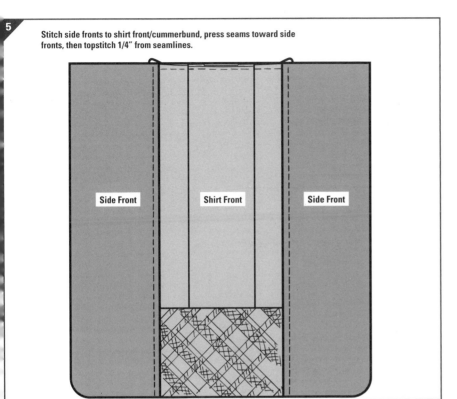

Side Front | Shirt Front | Side Front

■ Right sides together, fold the ribbing in half so the short edges meet; stitch the short edges together in a ¼" seam and press the seam open. Wrong sides together and raw edges matching, fold the ribbing in half lengthwise (Figure 7).

7

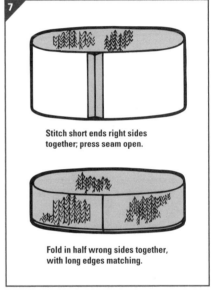

Stitch short ends right sides together; press seam open.

Fold in half wrong sides together, with long edges matching.

■ Wrong sides together, stitch the bib to the 12"x18" black cotton rectangle (lining), stitching a scant ¼" from the raw edges. Bind the raw edges with bias tape, beginning and ending at the center back (Figure 6).

■ Fold the bib at the bib front/back seamline.

■ Cut a 5 ¼"-diameter circle paper pattern for the neck opening, fold it in half, then center it on the folded bib, matching folds; cut out the neck opening. Stitch around the opening a scant ¼" from the raw edge.

6

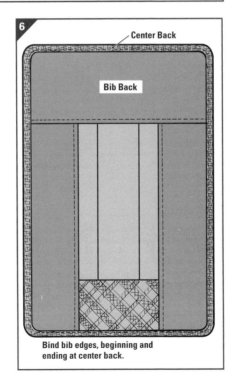

Center Back

Bib Back

Bind bib edges, beginning and ending at center back.

■ Divide the ribbing into quarters, using the seam as one marking, and mark with a water-soluble marker. Divide the bib neckline into quarters, beginning at the center back; mark.

■ Right sides together and raw edges matching, pin the ribbing to the neckline, with the ribbing seam matching the neckline's center back marking; match the remaining quarter markings accordingly. Stitch or serge in a ¼" seam, stretching the ribbing to fit between the quarter markings as you sew. If sewing on a conventional machine, zigzag stitch around the neckline again to finish.

■ Right sides facing, stitch the bow tie pieces together in a ¼" seam, leaving an opening for turning. Turn right side out, press and slipstitch the opening closed.

■ Easestitch across the tie center from long edge to long edge, and draw up the gathers as tightly as possible (Figure 8).

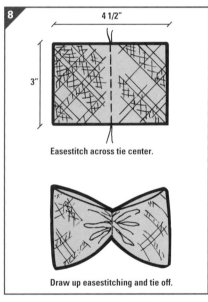

Easestitch across tie center.

Draw up easestitching and tie off.

■ Cut a 1½" x 2" rectangle of plaid, turn in the 2" raw edges to meet in the center and press. Fold the strip in half lengthwise and edgestitch close to both long edges (Figure 9).

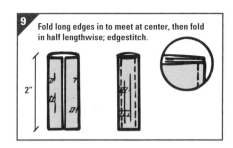

■ Wrap this strip around the bias side of the bow tie and tack in place on the back side. Hand tack the bow tie to the center front neckline seam and evenly space and hand stitch the buttons on the shirt front (Figure 10).

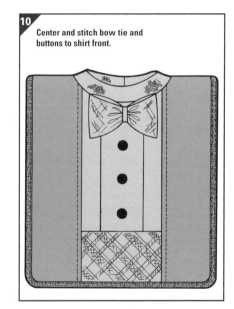

Center and stitch bow tie and buttons to shirt front.

GERRY GIRAFFE

For moms suffering through the trials and tribulations of their little one's teething, the teething ring attached to this bib is a real winner.

MATERIALS

- 18" x 26" rectangle of yellow terry cloth
- Scraps of firmly woven cotton fabric in green, red and bright yellow
- 6" square of fusible transfer web
- Two hook-and-loop dot fasteners
- 3" of ½"-wide rainbow-striped ribbon
- 2½ yards of blue double-fold bias tape
- Matching thread
- Pattern tracing cloth
- Primary-colored teething ring

CONSTRUCTION

■ Apply fusible transfer web to the wrong side of each fabric scrap.

■ Enlarge the patterns in Figure 11, page 93, and cut two bibs from the terry cloth. From the green fabric, cut one grass piece; from the yellow fabric, cut one head and one body; and from the red fabric, cut two ¾"-diameter circles, two ¼"-diameter circles and three 1⅛"-sided triangles for the giraffe feet, horns and spots, respectively.

■ Stitch the bibs wrong sides together a scant ¼" from all raw edges.

■ Bind the bib edges with bias tape, beginning and ending at one back neck end. *Note:* See "Applying Bias Binding" on page 83 for instructions on applying bias binding.

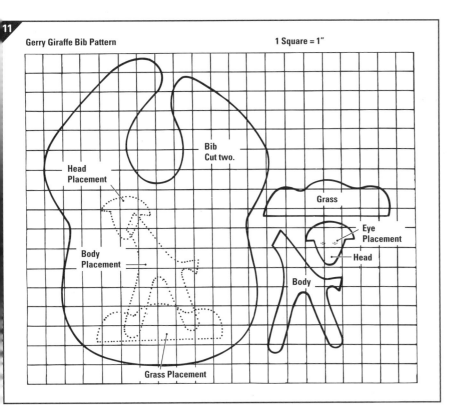

11

Gerry Giraffe Bib Pattern   1 Square = 1"

Head Placement

Bib Cut two.

Grass

Eye Placement

Head

Body Placement

Body

Grass Placement

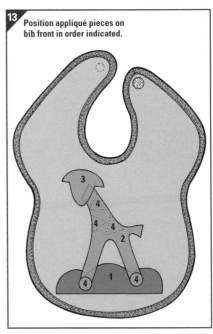

13 Position appliqué pieces on bib front in order indicated.

around   each   to   finish (Figure 14).

■ Apply the loop portion of the hook-and-loop fastener to the right side of the shorter neck end, the hook portion to the underside of the remaining neck end (Figure 12).

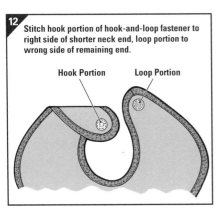

12 Stitch hook portion of hook-and-loop fastener to right side of shorter neck end, loop portion to wrong side of remaining end.

Hook Portion   Loop Portion

■ Remove the paper backing from the appliqué pieces, position them in the numerical order indicated in Figure 13, then fuse in place. To appliqué in place, satin stitch over the edges of each piece in the same order, changing the top thread as necessary to match each appliqué. *Note:* For helpful hints on satin stitching, see "Super Satin Stitching" on page 76.

■ Fuse the horns in place approximately ½" above the head and ¾" apart. Make a row of red satin stitches from the head up to each horn, then

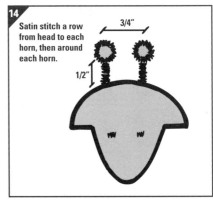

14 Satin stitch a row from head to each horn, then around each horn.

3/4"

1/2"

■ Using blue thread and following the placement markings on the head pattern, satin stitch the eyes.

■ Press under ¼" at each end of the ribbon. Position one portion of the hook-and-loop fastener at the fold and over the raw edge at each end and stitch in place (Figure 15). Position the ribbon on the completed bib and stitch one end in place (Figure 16). Attach the teething ring.

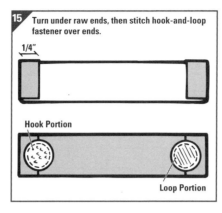

15 Turn under raw ends, then stitch hook-and-loop fastener over ends.

1/4"

Hook Portion

Loop Portion

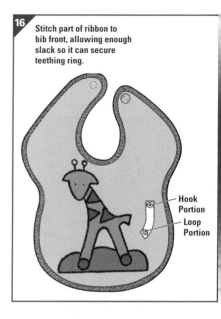

16 Stitch part of ribbon to bib front, allowing enough slack so it can secure teething ring.

Hook Portion

Loop Portion

— OPPOSITES ATTRACT —

Because of its endless versatility, hook-and-loop tape, such as Velcro®, is one of today's most widely used closures. It works anywhere two edges overlap—simply touch the two portions together and the hooks and loops interlock for a secure closure.

Available in circles, squares and strips in sew-on, adhesive-backed and iron-on varieties, hook-and-loop fasteners are not only popular for sportswear and home decor, but for children's clothing and accessories as well.

For the best results on all types of hook-and-loop fasteners, follow these tips:
■ Place the hook portion of the fastener outward, away from the body; place the loop (softer) portion inward, toward the body.
■ Angle the fastener corners to eliminate sharp points.
■ Close the hook-and-loop fastener when washing or dry cleaning an item to prevent the hooks from snagging other clothing and lint from collecting in the loops.

■ For the sew-on hook-and-loop fastener, also consider the following:
• Use glue stick to position the fastener before stitching it in place.
• Use a size 14 or 16 sewing machine needle.
• Edgestitch the fastener portions in place with a stitch length of 8 to 10 stitches per inch (2.5mm to 3mm long).
• When sewing a strip in place, begin near the center of one long edge and stitch around the strip, overlapping the stitches at the beginning and end (Figure 1).

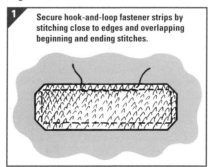

1 Secure hook-and-loop fastener strips by stitching close to edges and overlapping beginning and ending stitches.

• When sewing a circle in place, stitch in a triangle or square shape (Figure 2).

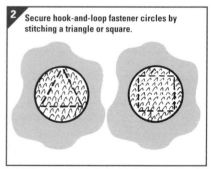

2 Secure hook-and-loop fastener circles by stitching a triangle or square.

PARTY PERFECT

When her party frock is just too pretty to muss, cover it with this lace-collared bib—she'll be the belle of the ball, and no one will be the wiser.

MATERIALS

● 13"x19" rectangle of firmly woven cotton fabric (print or solid)

● 13"x19" rectangle of white terry cloth

● 12" square of lace fabric

● 1½ yards of ½"-wide ruffled lace trim (to match lace fabric)

● 2½"x13" rectangle of white rib knit

● 1 yard of ⅛"-wide satin ribbon (to complement cotton fabric)

● Matching thread

● Pattern tracing cloth

CONSTRUCTION

■ Enlarge the pattern in Figure 17 and cut one collar from the lace fabric, cutting on the fold.

■ Right sides facing, stitch the 13"x19" cotton and terry cloth rectangles together in a ½" seam, rounding the corners and leaving a 3" opening along one long edge for turning (Figure 18). Trim the seam, turn right side out and press, pressing in the edges at the opening; edgestitch around the bib.

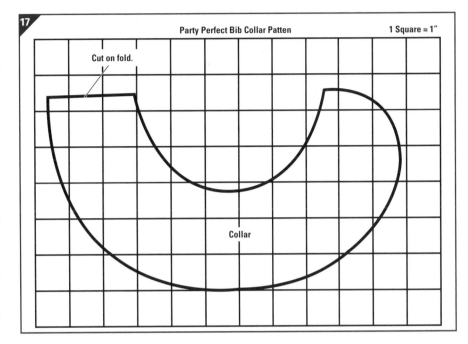

17 Party Perfect Bib Collar Patten   1 Square = 1"

Cut on fold.

Collar

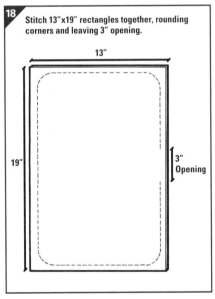

18 Stitch 13"x19" rectangles together, rounding corners and leaving 3" opening.

13"

19"

3" Opening

■ Turn down 5" at one short end of the bib and press lightly; this will be the bib upper edge. Cut a neck opening and stitch around it as for the tuxe-

do bib ("Mr. Irresistible") above.

■ Right side up, lap the lace trim finished edge ¼" over the lace collar outer edge; zigzag in place (Figure 19).

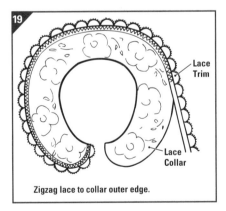

19

Lace Trim

Lace Collar

Zigzag lace to collar outer edge.

■ Place the collar on the bib right side, with the collar's inner curve matching the bib's neckline opening; stitch in place (Figure 20, page 96).

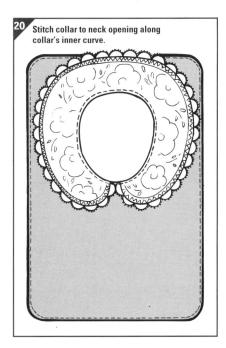

20 Stitch collar to neck opening along collar's inner curve.

■ Cut and apply the neckline ribbing to the neck opening as

for the tuxedo bib ("Mr. Irresistible") above.

■ Cut the ribbon in half; treating the two pieces as one, tie a bow and tack it to the bib center front neckline (Figure 21).

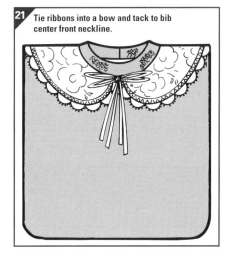

21 Tie ribbons into a bow and tack to bib center front neckline.

❑

— ZIP ZAP —

The next time you're unable to find the exact zipper length you need for a particular project—children's or otherwise—shorten a zipper! It's easy to do from either the top (done *after* the zipper is applied and the preferred method for skirts or pants with waistbands) or the bottom (done *before* the zipper is applied and recommended for any garment or project).

■ To shorten a zipper from the top:
• Apply the zipper, positioning the bottom stop at the placket opening lower edge.
• Open the zipper to avoid later cutting off the zipper tab.
• Stitch across the zipper tape at the desired zipper upper edge location within the seam allowance; cut off the excess zipper (Figure 1).
• Continue constructing the garment; the waistband or neckline facing will serve as the zipper top stop.

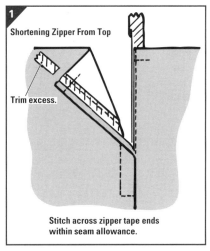

1 Shortening Zipper From Top

Trim excess.

Stitch across zipper tape ends within seam allowance.

■ To shorten a zipper from the bottom:

• From the top stop, mark the desired finished length of the zipper.
• To make a new bottom stop, hand whipstitch or machine zigzag over the zipper teeth at the desired finished length. Cut off the zipper ½" below the new bottom stop (Figure 2).

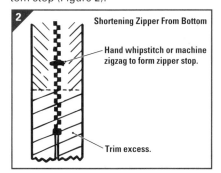

2 Shortening Zipper From Bottom

Hand whipstitch or machine zigzag to form zipper stop.

Trim excess.

• Apply the zipper. ❑

for photo finished projects on page 17

banded beauty

Few babies are graced with those precious locks of hair upon arrival, making the "Isn't he cute" statement a prevalent one to new mothers of boys and girls alike—a little distressing to many a new mom showing off her little princess. So, armed with a tiny wardrobe of clothing and accessories—all radiating pink, pink, pink—she waits for the day her daughter has enough hair to don a barrette or even a Velcro®-attached ribbon to tell the world that she's all girl!

In the meantime, look to this feminine but practical option: a tiny stretch lace headband embellished with a bow. This prim little hair (head) ornament doesn't attach to the hair but slips around the head.

And it's so simple even a novice fashion-sewer can complete one for a newborn or infant (six to 12 months) in just minutes.

NEWBORN HEADBAND

MATERIALS
- 12" of ½"-wide stretch lace (lingerie lace is appropriate)
- 5" of 1"-wide ribbon
- 2" of ⅜"-wide ribbon to match or contrast with the 1"-wide ribbon
- Liquid seam sealant, such as Fray Check™

CONSTRUCTION
■ Overlap the ends of the stretch lace ½" and straight stitch a boxed X on the overlap area (Figure 1). *Note:* If your machine balks at sewing on stretch lace, back the lace with a piece of tear-away stabilizer to minimize stretching as you stitch; remove the stabilizer after stitching.

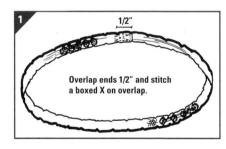
Overlap ends 1/2" and stitch a boxed X on overlap.

■ Fold the 1"-wide ribbon ends toward each other, overlapping them ½" at the center (Figure 2) for the bow; hand tack the overlap through all layers.

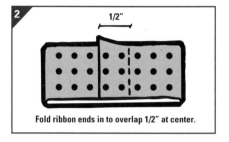
Fold ribbon ends in to overlap 1/2" at center.

■ With the bow and band right side up, stitch the bow center to the lace band overlap/seam through all layers (Figure 3).

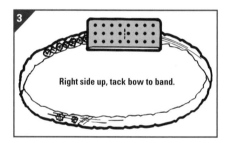
Right side up, tack bow to band.

■ Wrap the ⅜"-wide ribbon snugly around the bow center and elastic band for the bow knot, slightly gathering the bow. Tack the ends in place on the bow back side (Figure 4). Lightly coat the ribbon raw ends with seam sealant.

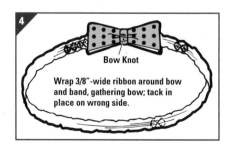
Bow Knot
Wrap 3/8"-wide ribbon around bow and band, gathering bow; tack in place on wrong side.

INFANT HEADBAND

MATERIALS

- 16" of ¼"-wide elastic
- 1¼ yards of ¾"-wide ribbon
- ⅓ yard of ⅛"-wide ribbon to match or contrast with the ¾"-wide ribbon
- Liquid seam sealant, such as Fray Check™

CONSTRUCTION

■ Cut a 27" length of the ¾"-wide ribbon. Lightly coat the raw ends with a liquid seam sealant.

■ Fold this piece of ribbon in half lengthwise, wrong sides together, and stitch close to the long edges, forming a tube.

■ Using a loop turner, bodkin or safety pin, pull the elastic through the ribbon tube, gathering the ribbon as necessary to fit the elastic. Overlap the elastic ends slightly and stitch them together to secure (Figure 5). Overlap the ribbon ends slightly and stitch them together to secure.

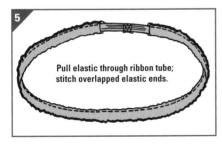

Pull elastic through ribbon tube; stitch overlapped elastic ends.

■ Cut the remaining ¾"-wide ribbon into two 9" lengths; lightly coat the raw ends with seam sealant. Form each into a figure-8 bow (Figure 6).

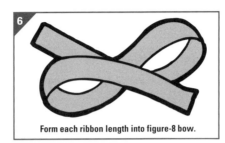

Form each ribbon length into figure-8 bow.

■ Right side up, place one figure-8 bow on top of the other, then secure and gather the centers with tiny hand stitches through all layers (Figure 7).

■ Cut two 6" lengths of the ⅛"-wide ribbon; lightly coat the raw ends of each with seam sealant, then form each into a figure-8 bow. Right side up, place one bow on top of the other, then place both on top of the larger-ribbon bow; hand stitch to secure.

Stack bows, then secure bow centers with small stitches.

■ Right side up, hand tack the completed bow to the band covering the band's seam. □

— INCHING ALONG —

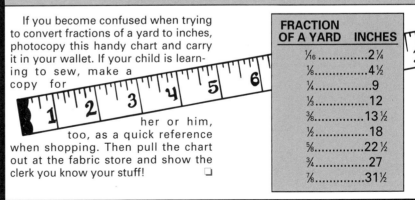

If you become confused when trying to convert fractions of a yard to inches, photocopy this handy chart and carry it in your wallet. If your child is learning to sew, make a copy for her or him, too, as a quick reference when shopping. Then pull the chart out at the fabric store and show the clerk you know your stuff! □

FRACTION OF A YARD	INCHES
¹⁄₁₆	2¼
⅛	4½
¼	9
⅓	12
⅜	13½
½	18
⅝	22½
¾	27
⅞	31½

for photo finished project on page 16

bitty book bag

This colorful, pint-sized version of Mom's backpack is one any child will love. Mix and match the sections in brightly colored pack cloth to make a sturdy bag with room for school books, a nutritious lunch and all the extras kids tote to school each day. The bag even features a special outer pocket for pencils, permission slips and bus or snack money. Let your child help choose the fabric colors to complement his or her style, then sew this one-of-a-kind backpack with minimal effort.

MATERIALS

• ½ yard of printed pack cloth
• ½ yard of solid-colored pack cloth to contrast with the print
• 6"x12" rectangle of solid-colored pack cloth to coordinate with the print for the pocket
• 6"x12" rectangle of mediumweight, fusible weft-insertion interfacing
• 1 yard of ¼"-diameter cording for covering your own piping or 1 yard of ready-made piping to coordinate with the pack cloth
• 1 yard of wide, double-fold bias tape to coordinate with the pack cloth
• 2 yards of 1"-wide nylon webbing to coordinate with the pack cloth
• Two ½"x1" rectangular rings or D-rings
• 12 ⅜"-diameter grommets
• Two 1"-square hook-and-loop tape fasteners
• Matching thread
• Pattern tracing cloth

CUTTING/CONSTRUCTION

Note: Use ½"-wide seam allowances throughout.

■ Enlarge the pattern pieces in Figure 1. From the print pack cloth, cut two upper flaps, two pocket flaps, two bag bottoms, one 1½"x36" drawstring strip and one 1½"x36" bias strip if you plan to make your own piping. From the contrasting solid pack cloth, cut two 14"x15" bag body rectangles.

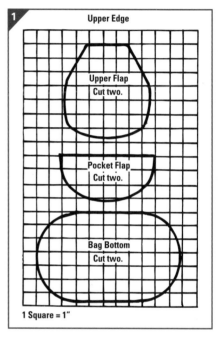

1

Upper Edge

Upper Flap
Cut two.

Pocket Flap
Cut two.

Bag Bottom
Cut two.

1 Square = 1"

■ Apply the interfacing to the 6"x12" pack cloth rectangle (pocket) wrong side, following the manufacturer's instructions.

■ Serge- or zigzag-finish both 6" edges and one 12" edge of the pocket. Press under ¼", then ½", along the remaining 12" edge (pocket upper edge), then stitch close to the first fold; press under the seam allowances on the finished edges, mitering the corners (Figure 2, page 100).

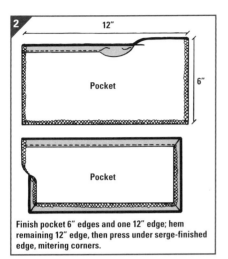

Finish pocket 6" edges and one 12" edge; hem remaining 12" edge, then press under serge-finished edge, mitering corners.

■ Center and pin the pocket right side up on one bag body rectangle (bag front) right side, with the pocket's side edges 3½" from the bag front 15" edges and 1½" from the bag front lower edge; edgestitch in place along the pocket side edges only (Figure 3). *Note:* The pocket slack created will be removed with pleats.

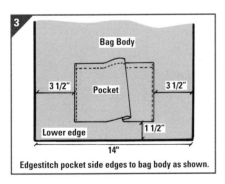

Edgestitch pocket side edges to bag body as shown.

■ Make two ¾"-deep pleats at the pocket lower side edges, removing the pocket slack; pin or baste in place, then edgestitch the pocket lower edge through all thicknesses, securing the pleats and the

lower edge to the bag body (Figure 4).

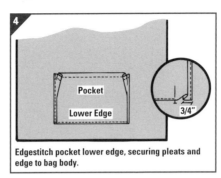

Edgestitch pocket lower edge, securing pleats and edge to bag body.

■ Baste the pocket flaps wrong sides together and treat them as one flap. Encase the flap's curved edge in double-fold bias tape (see "Applying Bias Binding" on page 83 for instructions on applying bias tape).

■ Serge- or zigzag-finish the flap's raw edge, then press under the seam allowance (Figure 5).

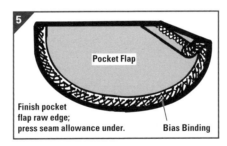

Finish pocket flap raw edge; press seam allowance under.   Bias Binding

■ Pin the pocket flap to the bag front just above the pocket upper edge; edgestitch the pocket flap upper edge in place.

■ Center and stitch the loop portion of a hook-and-loop tape fastener to the pocket flap underside, just inside the bias binding; center and stitch the

hook portion to the pocket right side approximately 1" from the pocket upper edge so the fastener portions meet when the flap is closed (Figure 6).

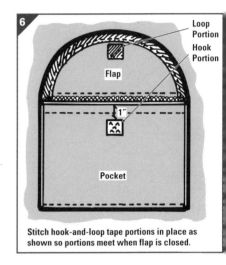

Stitch hook-and-loop tape portions in place as shown so portions meet when flap is closed.

■ Right sides together, stitch the bag front to the remaining bag body rectangle (back); serge- or zigzag-finish the raw edges and press them to one side. Press under ¼", then 1½", along the bag upper edge, then stitch close to both folds for the hem (Figure 7).

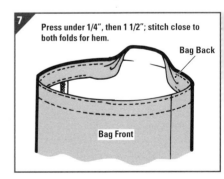

Press under 1/4", then 1 1/2"; stitch close to both folds for hem.

■ Baste the bag bottoms wrong sides together and treat them as one bag bottom. If you're covering your own piping, wrap the bias strip around the cording, with the bias strip wrong sides together and raw edges matching. Raw edges matching, pin this piece to the bag bottom, then, using a zipper foot to get as close to the cording as possible, machine baste in place for piping, clipping the piping seam allowances as necessary and turning in and overlapping the raw ends (Figure 8). If you're using ready-made piping, simply place the piping and bag bottom right sides together with raw edges matching and baste in place, using a zipper foot to get as close to the piping as possible, clipping the piping seam allowances as necessary and turning in and overlapping the raw ends.

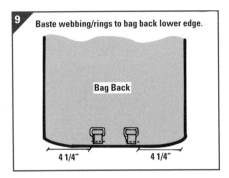

9 Baste webbing/rings to bag back lower edge.

Bag Back

4 1/4"   4 1/4"

■ Right sides together and raw edges even (with the piping sandwiched in between), pin the bag bottom to the bag body lower edge, positioning the bag bottom piping overlap at the bag center back; stitch in place just inside the piping basting line (Figure 10).

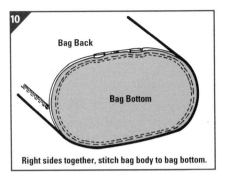

10

Bag Back

Bag Bottom

Right sides together, stitch bag body to bag bottom.

■ Press under the seam allowance along each upper flap's upper edge. Position the upper flaps wrong sides together and baste along the curved edges only; encase the curved edges in double-fold bias tape (see "Applying Bias Binding" on page 83 for

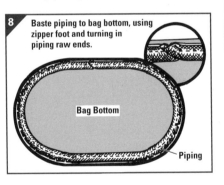

8 Baste piping to bag bottom, using zipper foot and turning in piping raw ends.

Bag Bottom

Piping

■ Cut two 3"-long pieces of nylon webbing and thread each through a rectangular ring; machine baste the raw edges together.

■ Raw edges matching, position and baste each webbing/ring at the bag back lower edge 4¼" from one side seam (Figure 9).

— SHORTENING A JACKET ZIPPER —

If you just can't find the correct length of separating jacket zipper you need, never fear...buy a slightly longer one and shorten it!

■ Separating zippers may be shortened *only* at the top, so stitch the zipper into the jacket as directed, allowing the excess length to extend at the neckline edge.

■ Partially open the zipper and place the slider 2" below the desired finished length to avoid detaching the slider.

■ If your zipper has a metal stop at the upper end, remove it with pliers and reposition it at the new length. If the stop is molded plastic, create a new one by whipstitching over the coil or teeth at the new desired length on each side of the zipper, then cut away the excess zipper tape ¾" above the new stop (Figure 1).

■ Finish the jacket.   ❏

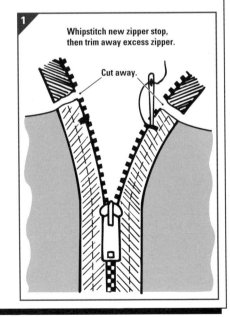

1 Whipstitch new zipper stop, then trim away excess zipper.

Cut away.

instructions on applying bias tape) (Figure 11). *Note:* The flaps's upper edges are not yet attached.

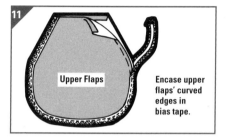

Encase upper flaps' curved edges in bias tape.

Upper Flaps

■ Center the upper flaps on the bag back right side, with the flaps' upper edges 2¼" from the bag back upper edge; pin the *lower layer only* of the flaps' upper edges to the bag back; baste in place (Figure 12).

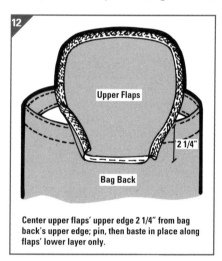

Upper Flaps

2 1/4"

Bag Back

Center upper flaps' upper edge 2 1/4" from bag back's upper edge; pin, then baste in place along flaps' lower layer only.

■ Cut the remaining nylon webbing into two equal lengths for straps. Tuck ½" of one end of each strap end between the upper flaps' turned edges, with the straps ¾" apart; baste. Edgestitch across the flaps' upper edge, securing the straps, then stitch

again ¼" from the edgestitching (Figure 13).

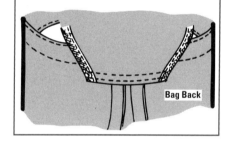

Bag Back

Tuck straps between upper flaps' turned edges, with straps 3/4" apart; baste. Edgestitch across flaps' upper edges, then 1/4" from edgestitching.

Bag Back

■ Center and stitch the loop portion of a hook-and-loop tape fastener to the upper flap underside just inside the bias binding; center and stitch the hook portion on the bag front approximately 1½" from the bag front upper edge so the fastener portions meet when the flap is closed.

■ Following the manufacturer's instructions, apply the grommets to the bag upper edge between the hem stitching rows in the locations indicated in Figure 14. *Note:* Grommet spacing is the same on the bag front and back.

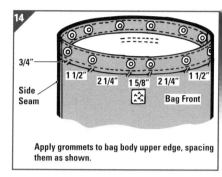

3/4"

Side Seam

1 1/2"   2 1/4"   1 5/8"   2 1/4"   1 1/2"

Bag Front

Apply grommets to bag body upper edge, spacing them as shown.

■ Fold the drawstring strip in half lengthwise, right sides together and press; unfold the strip. Press the strip long edges in to meet at the center foldline, then fold the strip in half again along the foldline, encasing the raw edges; press, then edgestitch along both long edges (Figure 15).

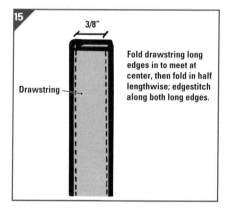

3/8"

Drawstring

Fold drawstring long edges in to meet at center, then fold in half lengthwise; edgestitch along both long edges.

■ Beginning at the bag center front outside, thread the drawstring through the grommets; knot each drawstring end (Figure 16, page 103).

■ Thread the remaining end of each webbing strap through its corresponding rectangular ring at the bag back lower edge and pin in place as shown in Figure 17, page 103.

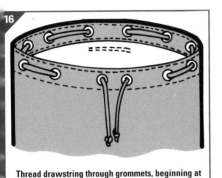

16

Thread drawstring through grommets, beginning at bag center front outside; knot ends.

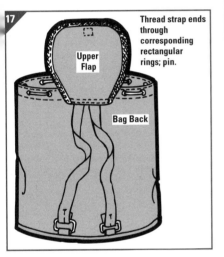

17

Thread strap ends through corresponding rectangular rings; pin.

Upper Flap

Bag Back

■ Have the child try on the bag and adjust the strap length for a comfortable fit; re-pin, then trim away excess webbing, if necessary. Use a closely spaced zigzag stitch to finish each strap raw end, then secure each strap end in place with two rows of closely spaced straight stitching. ❏

— RUFFLING MADE EASY —

To add a touch of softness and/or femininity to your decorating projects, add a ruffle. The following instructions are for a 1¼"-wide ruffle, but the width can be modified, depending on the size needed.

■ Cut and piece enough 3½"-wide fabric strips to create a strip one and one-half to two times the necessary finished ruffle length, depending upon the desired ruffle fullness.

■ Fold the ruffling strip in half lengthwise, right sides together. Stitch each strip end in a ½" seam, then turn the strip right side out.

■ Divide the ruffling strip into quarters along the raw edges; mark with a small clip. Repeat along the raw edge to which the ruffle will be applied—a bumper pad, for example (Figure 1).

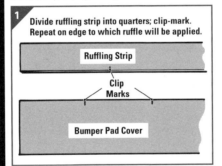

1
Divide ruffling strip into quarters; clip-mark. Repeat on edge to which ruffle will be applied.

Ruffling Strip

Clip Marks

Bumper Pad Cover

■ Cut a piece of pearl cotton, dental floss, string or another cording the length

of the ruffle, then zigzag over the cording ⅜" from the ruffle raw edges; do not allow the stitching to pierce the cording (Figure 2).

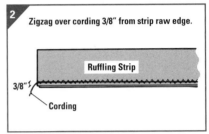

2
Zigzag over cording 3/8" from strip raw edge.

Ruffling Strip

3/8"

Cording

■ Right sides together, pin the ruffle to the edge of its respective piece, matching clip marks. Pull the cording to adjust the gathers evenly; pin. (Figure 3). Machine baste ½" from the raw edges to secure the ruffle.

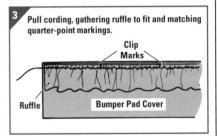

3
Pull cording, gathering ruffle to fit and matching quarter-point markings.

Clip Marks

Ruffle

Bumper Pad Cover

■ Complete the project, following its instructions. ❏

KIDS CAN SEW, TOO!

Curiosity. A desire to learn. Unbridled enthusiasm. Few inhibitions. Juvenile creativity. These are just a few of the characteristics our children possess which make them absolutely wonderful candidates for budding fashion-sewers.

It is possible, you know, to teach even very young children the joys of sewing. And lets face it, children are tiny beings who love to create. What better way to indulge this innocence and enthusiasm than to inspire our children to sew. It's a skill they will use over the course of their life—in many, many ways. For example, what begins with sewing doll clothes for a favorite Barbie® could someday lead to a career in fashion design. And introducing young boys to sewing will help them in wardrobing (selection and care) throughout their lives, fostering both independence and self-esteem.

Besides offering you detailed guidelines on inspiring and teaching your child to sew ("Keeping Children In Stitches"), you'll find a few simple project ideas, ranging from very simple to simple. The chapter even touches on introducing children to the fascinating serger ("Serger Kids"), whetting their appetite with inspiration for serging an easy-to-construct sweatshirt any child would adore.

"Sew Gifted" features five quick-and-easy designs kids can sew as gifts or for themselves. A few of these include an uncomplicated doll sleeping bag (perfect for that cherished baby doll or Cabbage Patch) for sis, and a kitchen towel caddy for Mom.

For the little guy, "Tool Cool" is a simple shop apron, complete with a tool "belt" for accommodating a small hammer, wrench, pliers, etc. This will be equally at home in shop class or Dad's workroom.

These and other projects throughout SEWING KIDS' STUFF will peak your child's interest in sewing, creating and building his or her own sense of style. So, go ahead and indulge your kids, offering them the opportunity to learn this skill so precious to you for a lifetime of creative fulfillment. ❏

keeping children in stitches

If you've ever considered teaching your child to sew, only to dismiss the idea for fear you'd both end up frustrated and dwelling on the negatives, take heart. Instead of teaching, consider *inspiring* your child to sew. He or she will then *want* to learn the specifics of sewing and growing—to be taught by you or another qualified teacher.

This will allow your child to gain from you something more important than exact sewing techniques: the sense of accomplishment and joy of creativity sewing can bring. A wise man once said, "The mediocre teacher tells, the good teacher explains, the superior teachers demonstrates and the great teacher *inspires*." Based on our own experiences, this probably rings true for many individuals.

Fashion-sewing experts have ideas for inspiring kids to sew, and being an expert seamstress is *not* a prerequisite. A positive attitude is. Your enthusiasm will not only be encouraging, but contagious as well.

The following dos and don'ts will provide you with a solid foundation on which to base your inspirational plan.

DOS

■ Begin with sewing projects appropriate to your child's age, interests, abilities and skill level.

For example, allow very young children the benefit of sewing on fabric stretched taut in an embroidery hoop instead of loose fabric. And let children sew what they want to sew—maybe blankets and pillows for a Barbie® doll, a simple elasticized-waist A-line skirt, a horse blanket or a simple pair of sweats, depending on their interests.

■ Start the very young child with cutting. The process of making straight and curved cuts on fabric, playing with the shapes, then wrapping the fabric around a doll or toy and seeing it in its three dimensions is very educational.

■ Share the experience of sewing when possible. For example, if you're sewing an outfit for your child, allow him or her to help you cut it out and finish it. Keep in mind this won't be as efficient as sewing the entire project yourself, but the experience for your child could prove invaluable. Remember, though, to avoid giving the child dull sewing jobs, which might dampen the spirit.

■ Allow the learner to do the work, but be sure to help with any necessary ripping to avoid too much discouragement when faced with correcting an error.

■ Encourage proper use of the sewing machine, and be sure to supervise younger children at the machine. A good introduction to correct posture, speed control and fabric placement can help prevent frustration and eliminate mistakes.

■ Take your child shopping and use this opportunity to talk about fabric, pattern and notion choices. Selecting these elements is a very important part of the creative process.

■ Provide children with choices and allow them to make decisions. In the process, they should learn the difference between "good" and "better." Do not provide the child with poor choices as a learning tool, however. It's disheartening for a child to learn the "hard way."

■ Encourage proper use of the pattern, especially reading and following the guidesheet.

■ Encourage children to make small gifts for relatives or teachers. This allows the child to show off his or her work and experience pride in finished projects.

■ Encourage your child's creativity, keeping in mind there is more than one way to do almost anything.

DON'TS

■ Avoid shutting your child out of the sewing room, regardless of how busy you are. Watching you sew, even under pressure, will inspire a curiosity about the process and instill in the child that sewing is something worthwhile, enjoyable and challenging. Even a toddler can have fun playing with ribbon scraps or cutting fabric scraps on your sewing room floor.

■ Don't hover over your child while he or she sews. Let the child discover sewing.

■ Do not nitpick. Although it will be difficult to stand back and allow mistakes to occur, this luxury of responsibility and independence will make the process much more of a pleasure than a chore for the child.

■ Avoid frustrating the child with scissors that won't cut, needles with eyes too tiny to thread, worn out marking pens, a machine that skips stitches, etc. Be sure all your sewing equipment and notions are in working order—the child is facing enough obstacles without these avoidable irritants.

■ Don't always insist your child finish every project—keep in mind the value of the process. Threatening that you won't buy any more materials until a project is complete could dampen the spirit. And we all know that sewing doesn't necessarily mean *finishing* every project—as much as we would like it to!

■ Don't purchase a toy sewing machine for your child and expect the child to use it for anything other than playing. If you don't want to share your own machine, purchase a less expensive or used model specifically for your child.

■ Don't forget the need of immediate gratification for younger and older kids. Allow them to make some things that can be finished quickly. Simple projects, such as tiny toy totes

for youngsters or laundry bags for teens require little fabric, little time and cause little frustration.

■ Don't attempt to teach your child to sew out of obligation. Instead approach the task with a sense of confidence and enthusiasm.

TIME TO TEACH

When you've inspired your child to take an interest in sewing and you're ready to indulge in the specifics of teaching this special skill, the following tips will help.

■ Determine your child's motor skill level and hand-eye coordination to thread a needle, knot a thread end, pin a pattern and sew a relatively straight seam on the sewing machine. Then, focus on the child's area(s) of strength while he or she develops the other areas.

■ Determine how long your child will be content to work on a specific project, then limit your sewing sessions to this time frame.

— KID-BITS —

Before the introduction of ready-to-wear clothing (late 19th century), all girls learned to sew at an early age, beginning with samplers and doll clothes.

■ Supply the child with the proper sewing notions *before* beginning a project. These include the following:

● Fabric

● Pattern

● Thread—one color to match fabric, another contrasting color for basting

● Sharp scissors

● Sewing needles with large eyes for easy threading

● Long straight pins, such as quilting pins, for easy maneuvering

● Pin cushion

● Thimble to fit the middle finger

● Marking devices, such as chalk and water-soluble markers

● Tape measure with numbers on both sides

● Seam ripper

● Shoe box to hold supplies

● Sewing machine

■ Help your child select patterns that are simple, fun, functional and can be completed in a short period of time. Then encourage your child to plan to add simple embellishments to the finished projects to make them unique. A fun first project is a pin cushion—something the child can finish in one sewing session and use for subsequent sewing.

■ Fabric should be as important a consideration for a child's sewing project as it is for your own. Recommended fabrics include mediumweight cottons or cotton blends and knits—if the child has access to a serger (see "Serger Kids" on page 121 for tips on teaching your child about this magical machine). Avoid silky fabrics and those with nap.

■ Be sure to conclude *every* sewing session with a success ful, happy child. Achieve this end result by keeping the elements simple—patterns, fabrics, projects and instructions —and your enthusiasm high. Allow choices and encourage deviations.

■ Most of all, remember: The best motivator to a learning child is recognition, so praise and acknowledge every accomplishment. This should keep your child in stitches for many years to come. ❏

— TODDLER SEWCOLOGY —

Toddlers are active, adventurous, curious and demanding. If it seems too difficult to make time for sewing unless they're sleeping, consider the following tactics. These approaches will not only let you accomplish your tasks at hand, but give you some creative time with your little one in the bargain.

■ Include the toddler in as many of your activities as possible so he or she will be willing to cooperate and let you sew. Let him or her explore the sewing machine without actually operating it to satisfy some curiosity. Children understand much earlier than most adults think they do, and they can certainly learn there's a time to touch and a time not to touch. And remember: Nothing is more attractive to a toddler than an item he or she is not allowed to touch.

■ If the child is young enough to stay in a baby seat, swing or playpen, keep this item right next to, but out of reach of, the sewing machine. This will allow you to keep an eye on each other. Let the child know sewing is your "special time," and playing nearby can be a special time for him or her, too. Perhaps a particular toy or two kept just for these occasions will help.

■ If the toddler is a bit older and able to reason, explain that sewing is something you like to do and insist the child entertain himself or herself for that period of time. But don't hesitate to stop occasionally and give a hug. It's important the child realizes sewing doesn't mean you're too busy to love him or her.

■ Don't try to hold a child on your lap while you sew. It's dangerous and encourages too much dependence and uncertainty.

■ If you can arrange to sew during a children's television program (entertainment or educational), place a small television set close to the sewing machine and set up a special space for your child to watch and still be near you. Demonstrating your special interests to your children will also encourage them to develop their interests, imaginations and independence. You'll all be happier in the long run. ❏

sew gifted

Gift giving is a significant part of many holidays, and for children it's especially momentous. But for as much as kids love *receiving* gifts, giving them has appeal, too. Help your child sew gifts to give—a bit of skill, basic sewing machine expertise and adult supervision are the only requisites needed for young children to sew gifts for every member of the family. Watching your youngster's face light up as he announces to the recipient, "I made it myself!" will make it all worthwhile.

DOLL/STUFFED ANIMAL SLEEPING BAG

MATERIALS
- ¾ yard of 44"-wide single-faced quilted fabric (this will yield two bags)
- ¾ yard of 44"-wide flannel or broadcloth for the lining to match the quilted fabric (this will yield two bags)
- ¾ yard of ⅜"-wide ribbon to coordinate with the fabric
- Matching thread

CONSTRUCTION
■ Cut the quilted fabric in half, creating two 22"x 27" rectangles for the bag body; repeat with the lining fabric for the lining. Set one rectangle of each fabric aside to make a second sleeping bag later, if desired.

■ On the lining rectangle, mark the center of each 22" edge with a ¼"-long clip into the seam allowance.

■ Right sides together and raw edges matching, pin the lining rectangle to the bag body rectangle.

■ Using a ⅝" seam allowance and working from the lining side, stitch around the bag outer edges from clip mark to clip mark, leaving the lower one-half of the bag unstitched (Figure 1); trim the seam and corners (diagonally) to ¼", turn the bag right side out and press.

■ Fold the bag in half widthwise, quilted fabric sides together, matching clips and raw edges; pin.

■ Using a ⅝" seam allowance, stitch the bag lower one-half from the clips to the folded edge (Figure 2); trim the seam

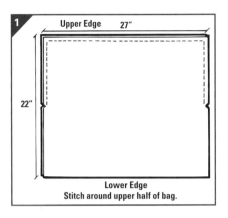

Figure 1 — Upper Edge 27" — 22" — Lower Edge — Stitch around upper half of bag.

and corners (diagonally) to ¼", turn the bag right side out and press.

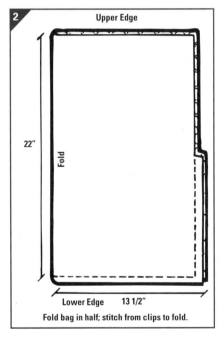

Figure 2 — Upper Edge — 22" — Fold — Lower Edge 13 1/2" — Fold bag in half; stitch from clips to fold.

■ Cut the ribbon into two 13½" pieces and tie each into a bow. Tack the bows on the sleeping bag edges as shown in Figure 3, page 110.

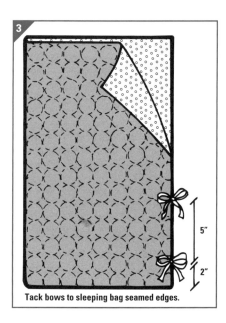

Tack bows to sleeping bag seamed edges.

NUGGET BELT

MATERIALS

- ¼ yard of 45"-wide felt or synthetic suede, such as Ultrasuede®, or leather scraps
- 2" of hook-and-loop tape, such as Velcro®
- Two 5" squares of cardboard
- Matching thread
- Rhinestones and rhinestone setter (optional)
- Gold or silver studs (optional)
- Glue-on sequins (optional)

CONSTRUCTION

Note: Embellishment on this belt design can be varied, depending on the child's age and skill level. For maximum results with minimal expertise, choose glue-on glittery sequins, studs or rhinestones.

Also keep in mind, using genuine leather may require extra adult stitching assistance.

■ Enlarge the nuggets in Figure 4, and cut one of each from cardboard for templates.

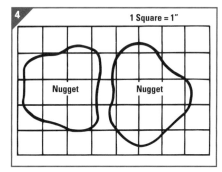

1 Square = 1"

Nugget   Nugget

■ Using the cardboard templates, trace an equal number of each nugget shape onto the felt or leather wrong side. *Note:* The number of nuggets needed will depend on the waist size of the intended wearer. For example, use 15 nuggets for a 22" to 24" waist size.

■ Shape the belt by positioning nuggets edge to edge as desired in a relatively straight line to a length about 4" shorter than the waist measurement, then add a set of approximately three nuggets to each end, curving one set up slightly, the other down slightly (Figure 5).

■ Join the nuggets by overlapping the edge of one over the edge of the next, turning the nuggets randomly as desired; edgestitch along each overlap (Figure 6).

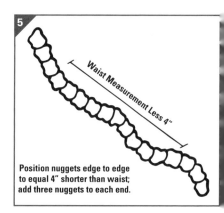

Position nuggets edge to edge to equal 4" shorter than waist; add three nuggets to each end.

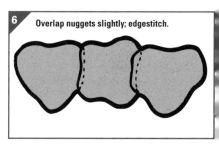

Overlap nuggets slightly; edgestitch.

■ Apply trimmings to the belt randomly as desired, following the manufacturer's instructions for setting rhinestones or studs or applying sequins.

■ Try on the belt and determine the waist or hip overlap; mark the closure location on the underlap and overlap.

■ Stitch the hook portion of hook-and-loop tape to the right side of one nugget at the belt underlap marking, the corresponding loop portion to the wrong side of one nugget at the belt overlap marking.

VARIATIONS

Encourage your child to vary this project to create special effects. Some ideas:

- Vary nugget shapes more dramatically.

- Use different colors for holiday or theme belts.

- Make the belt uneven at various points by lowering nuggets occasionally in a distinct pattern.

- Use blended shades of felt or Ultrasuede to complement different ensembles.

TOWEL CADDY

MATERIALS

- One hand towel (will yield two caddies)

- ¼ yard of decorator fabric

- One 2"x7" rectangle of contrasting fabric

- 1½" of ¾"-wide hook-and-loop tape, such as Velcro®

- One 1"-diameter button to match towel and fabric

- Matching thread

CONSTRUCTION

- Trace the caddy pattern in Figure 7 and cut two from the decorator fabric.

- Press under ⅝" along each caddy lower edge.

- Press under ½" along each long edge of the contrasting fabric rectangle.

- Pin the rectangle right side up on one caddy right side ⅝" from the lower edge; edgestitch in place along both long edges for the caddy front

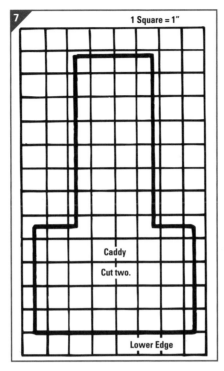

(Figure 8). Use decorative machine stitches for variety.

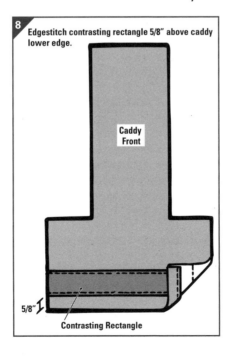

- Cut the hand towel in half widthwise, creating two terry cloth rectangles measuring approximately 13"x17" each (these dimensions will vary with towel brands); set one aside to make another towel caddy later, if desired.

- With the towel rectangle wrong side up, fold back each selvage edge 3"; pin to secure (Figure 9).

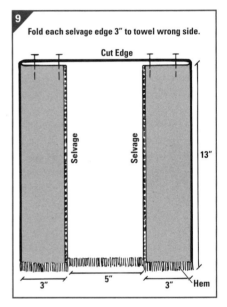

- Make a box pleat at the towel rectangle cut edge so it measures 7" across as shown in Figure 10, page 112, basting across the pleat to secure it.

- KID-BITS -

Until well into the 18th century, children were dressed like miniature adults, complete with such "fashionable" accessories as swords.

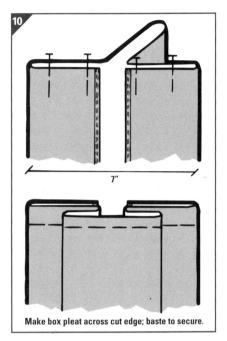

Make box pleat across cut edge; baste to secure.

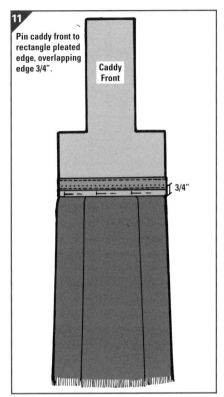

Pin caddy front to rectangle pleated edge, overlapping edge 3/4".

Caddy Front

3/4"

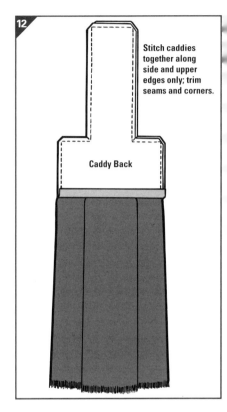

Stitch caddies together along side and upper edges only; trim seams and corners.

Caddy Back

■ With the caddy wrong side against the towel right side, pin the caddy front lower edge to the rectangle pleated edge, with the caddy overlapping the rectangle ¾" and side edges matching (Figure 11); baste.

■ Right sides together and raw edges matching, stitch the caddy front to the caddy back along the side and upper edges only in a ⅝" seam; trim the seams, clip the inner corners and trim the outer corners (diagonally) to ¼" (Figure 12).

■ Turn the caddy right side out and press; edgestitch across the caddy front lower edge, securing the caddy front, back and towel pleated edge (Figure 13, page 113).

— A+ D-RINGS —

The D-ring buckle is as versatile as it is fashionable. From a sport belt to the strap on a duffle bag, D-rings provide an easy-to-use, easily adjustable buckle for children's projects.

D-rings are available in widths ranging from ¾" to 2" in brass, gold and silver metallics, plus black, white and fashion colors to please any child.

To make your little one a quick, sporty belt, you'll need two D-rings, a clamp-on metal tip and webbing or stretch belting in the same width as the D-rings (to determine the necessary belting length, measure your child's waist, then add 6").

■ Insert one end of the belt through both D-rings and wrap it around the rings' straight sides.

■ Stitch securely, allowing enough room between the fold and the stitching for the rings to rest side by side. If the belting ravels, treat the ends with a seam sealant, such as Fray Check™.

■ Finish the remaining belting end with the clamp-on metal tip, following the manufacturer's instructions.

■ To buckle the belt, insert the metal tip through both D-rings, then back through one of them, as shown in the illustration. Pull the belting to fit. ❏

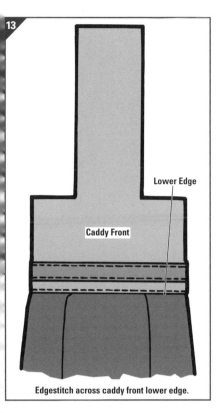

Edgestitch across caddy front lower edge.

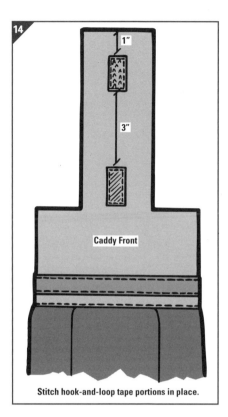

Stitch hook-and-loop tape portions in place.

■ Center and stitch the hook portion of the hook-and-loop tape 1" from the caddy front upper edge, the loop portion 3" below the hook portion (Figure 14).

■ Secure the hook-and-loop tape, then center and stitch a decorative button 1/2" from the caddy back upper edge (Figure 15).

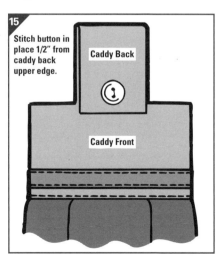

Stitch button in place 1/2" from caddy back upper edge.

— KID-BITS —

Victorian children's clothing, which included military uniforms, Highland (Scottish tartan) dress and sailor suits (which were so comfortable they became classic), often resembled fancy-dress costumes.

COSMETIC BAG

MATERIALS

- 10"x13" rectangle of single- or double-faced quilted fabric
- 10"x13" rectangle of vinyl or thin plastic sheeting (optional)
- One 12"-long matching zipper
- Matching thread
- Paper clips (optional)
- Sharp, size 12 (80) needle (optional)

CONSTRUCTION

Note: The vinyl lining on this simple-to-make bag is optional and may require additional adult assistance for inexperienced sewers, as vinyl has a tendency to stick to the sewing machine presser foot. A layer of tissue on top of the vinyl will make stitching smoother and more even, and using paper clips instead of pins will prevent small holes. Also, use a sharp, size 12 (80) needle and a slightly longer than normal stitch length.

The following instructions are for a lined bag; if you don't plan to line the bag, disregard all references to the vinyl.

■ Stitch the fabric and vinyl *wrong* sides together ¼" from all edges.

■ Right sides together and raw edges matching, position the zipper on the bag front along the 10" edges, with the zipper pull ¼" from the bag's 13" edge; stitch along the zipper's upper edge, using a zipper foot (Figure 16).

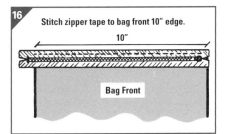

16 Stitch zipper tape to bag front 10" edge.

10"

Bag Front

■ Right sides together and raw edges matching, position the bag's remaining 10" edge along the zipper's remaining edge, with the zipper pull ¼" from the bag's 13" edge as above; stitch the zipper in place, using a zipper foot.

■ Trim the vinyl from the zipper seam allowances.

■ Turn the bag right side out, open the zipper and topstitch ¼" from the zipper along both edges, securing the seam allowances (Figure 17).

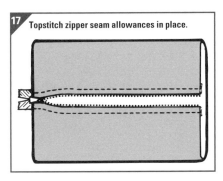

17 Topstitch zipper seam allowances in place.

■ Close the zipper and stitch across the extending end several times; cut off the excess length.

■ Open the zipper; right sides together, stitch the bag side edges in a ½" seam for 4½" below the zipper (Figure 18).

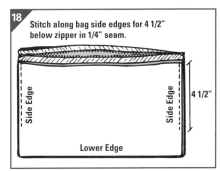

18 Stitch along bag side edges for 4 1/2" below zipper in 1/4" seam.

Side Edge

Side Edge

4 1/2"

Lower Edge

■ Make a small clip at each side edge/lower edge corner (Figure 19).

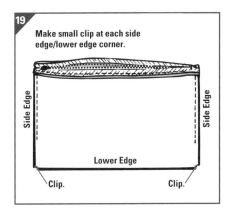

19 Make small clip at each side edge/lower edge corner.

Side Edge

Side Edge

Lower Edge

Clip.

Clip.

■ Flatten the bag lower edge and fold it into a T shape up to the side edge stitching; stitch across each end of the T, breaking the stitching and backstitching at each center clip, as shown in Figure 20. Trim the seams and clip corners (diagonally) to ¼".

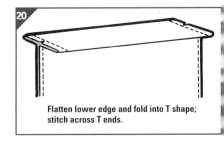

20

Flatten lower edge and fold into T shape; stitch across T ends.

■ If desired, overcast or serge-finish the seam allowances to neaten the bag inside.

■ Turn the bag right side out.

WINDSHIELD SCRAPER MITT

MATERIALS

• 7½" x 22" rectangle of synthetic suede, such as Ultrasuede® or leather

• 7½" x 22" rectangle of fake fur or shearling

• One ice scraper (10" maximum length, 3"-wide blade)

• Liquid seam sealant, such as Fray Check™

• Matching thread

CONSTRUCTION

■ Wrong sides together and raw edges matching, stitch the fake fur rectangle (lining) to the Ultrasuede rectangle (mitt) along the 7½" edges ¼" from the edges.

■ Measure across the scraper 2½" from the blade and measure the scraper's depth at this point (Figure 21, page 115); note these measurements.

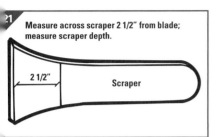

21 Measure across scraper 2 1/2" from blade; measure scraper depth.

2 1/2" — Scraper

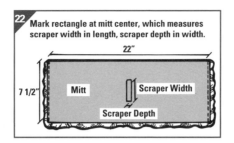

22 Mark rectangle at mitt center, which measures scraper width in length, scraper depth in width.

22"

7 1/2" — Mitt — Scraper Width — Scraper Depth

■ Working on the Ultrasuede side of the mitt, center and mark a rectangle the length of the scraper width and the width of the scraper depth Figure 22). Stitch on the marked rectangle through both ayers.

■ Slash the rectangle (both ayers) through the center and to each corner and cut out the center (Figure 23). Insert the scraper and test for fit, making the rectangle larger if necessary; remove the scraper.

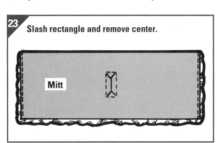

23 Slash rectangle and remove center.

Mitt

■ Apply seam sealant to the rectangle raw edges; reinsert the scraper and allow to dry.

■ Fold the mitt in half width-wise, lining sides together, and stitch along the raw edges in a ¼" seam; turn up the lower edge to form a lining (fake fur) cuff (Figure 24).

24 Stitch raw edges in 1/4" seam; turn up cuff at lower edge.

Mitt

Fake Fur Cuff

❏

— BIAS TAPE MADE EASY —

Making your own bias tape can be fast, easy and economical—plus, it can give your sewn creations a custom touch kids will love. And because these strips are cut on the bias (or at an angle), striped or printed fabric make especially unique trims.

Using the techniques below, you can cut more than 30 yards of 1"-wide bias from a single yard of 45"-wide fabric, using almost any fabric to match your bias trims to perfection.

■ For the best results, cut bias strips on the *true* bias fabric grain, which lies at a 45-degree angle to the selvage. This grain is very pliant, so it molds smoothly around curves and shaped edges, as well as corners and straight lines.

■ To determine the fabric's true bias grain, fold the fabric's cut crosswise edge to meet its lengthwise selvage edge (Figure 1); press the fold, which is the true bias grain.

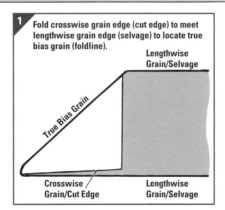

1 Fold crosswise grain edge (cut edge) to meet lengthwise grain edge (selvage) to locate true bias grain (foldline).

Lengthwise Grain/Selvage

True Bias Grain

Crosswise Grain/Cut Edge — Lengthwise Grain/Selvage

■ Use the bias fold as a guide for cutting a small quantity of bias strips. Measure and mark the cutting lines with chalk or a water-soluble marker, or use a rotary cutter and transparent ruler as your cutting guide.

■ Cut the bias strips twice the desired finished width, plus seam allowances. For example, cut 2 ½"-wide strips for 1"-wide bias tape with ¼" seam allowances.

■ To piece strips together:
• Right sides together, place one strip at a right angle to another strip, with diagonal cut ends matching (Figure 2).

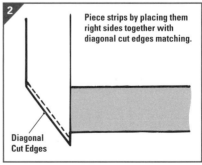

2 Piece strips by placing them right sides together with diagonal cut edges matching.

Diagonal Cut Edges

Continued on next page.

• Stitch the strips together in a ¼" seam; press the seam open.
• Trim away the extending points as shown (Figure 3).

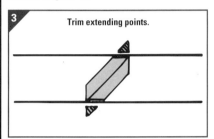

3 Trim extending points.

■ To cut a large quantity of bias strips, use the continuous bias strip method:
• Cut a perfect square from the fabric (the larger the square, the more bias tape it will produce).
• Draw a diagonal cutting line between two of the square's corners, forming two triangles; cut along this line, then number the cut edges with chalk or a water-soluble marker as shown (Figure 4).

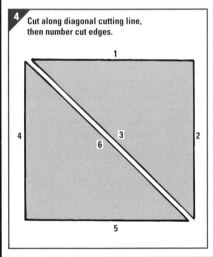

4 Cut along diagonal cutting line, then number cut edges.

• Right sides together, join edges No. 1 and No. 5 in a ¼" seam; press the seam open (Figure 5).

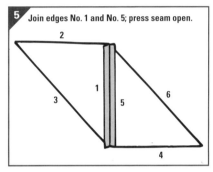

5 Join edges No. 1 and No. 5; press seam open.

• Mark the entire fabric with the desired width cutting lines for the bias strips, drawing the lines parallel to edges No. 6 and No. 3 (Figure 6). *Note:* If the last strip is an odd width which will not yield a complete strip, trim it away.

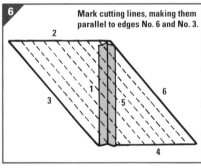

6 Mark cutting lines, making them parallel to edges No. 6 and No. 3.

• Right sides together, offset edges No. 2 and No. 4 by one bias strip width and stitch the edges together in a ¼" seam (Figure 7). *Note:* This will produce a slightly twisted fabric tube. Press the seam open.

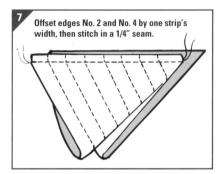

7 Offset edges No. 2 and No. 4 by one strip's width, then stitch in a 1/4" seam.

• To cut the strips, begin at one offset end and cut in a spiral, following the marked cutting lines (Figure 8).

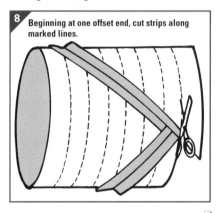

8 Beginning at one offset end, cut strips along marked lines.

tool cool

Every little handy-man needs his (or her!) own tool apron, complete with the essential, real-life tools to give Dad a hand around the shop. An adjustable neck cord allows this worktime accessory to fit sizes 6 to 10, and it's a snap to sew—perfect for a quick gift or novice sewer's first project.

MATERIALS

- ¾ yard of 45"-wide striped denim, ticking or canvas
- ⅞ yard of 45"-wide solid-colored denim to coordinate with the striped fabric
- 3 yards of ⅜"-diameter cable cording or ¾"-wide grosgrain ribbon to coordinate with the fabric
- Air- or water-soluble marker
- Matching thread

CUTTING

■ Enlarge the patterns in Figure 1. From the striped denim, cut one apron front; from the solid denim, cut one apron lining, two armhole facings, one 5"x12½" rectangle for the tool strap and enough 2"-wide true-bias strips to make a 1½-yard-long binding strip, piecing as necessary.

■ Transfer the tool section stitching lines to the tool strap right side and to the apron front right side (Figure 2, page 118).

CONSTRUCTION

Note: Use ½"-wide seam allowances throughout, unless otherwise noted.

■ *Wrong* sides together and side and lower raw edges matching, machine baste the apron front to the lining along the side and lower edges (Figure 3, page 118).

■ Press under ½" along the lining upper edge, then press under another ½", concealing the apron front upper raw edge; edgestitch along the lining's first fold to secure (Figure 4, page 118).

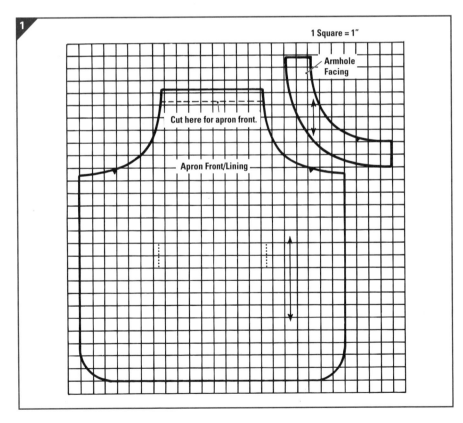

1 Square = 1"
Armhole Facing
Cut here for apron front.
Apron Front/Lining

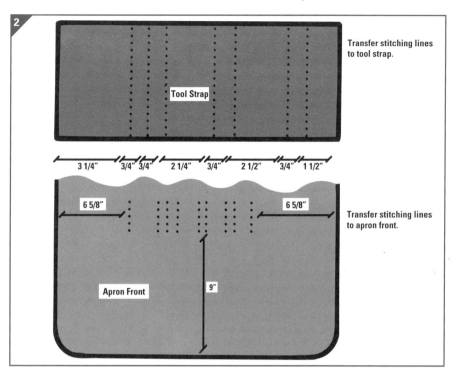

2

Transfer stitching lines to tool strap.

Tool Strap

3 1/4" | 3/4" | 3/4" | 2 1/4" | 3/4" | 2 1/2" | 3/4" | 1 1/2"

6 5/8"   6 5/8"

Transfer stitching lines to apron front.

Apron Front

9"

3

Baste front to lining along side and lower edges.

Apron Lining

Apron Front

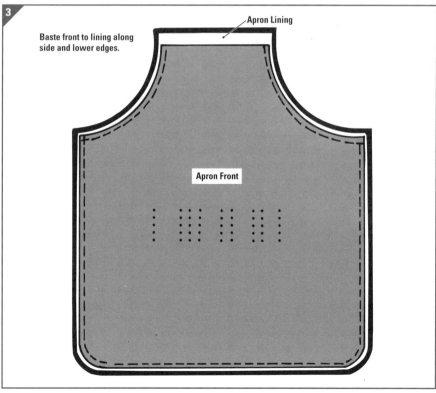

4

Apron Front
Upper Raw Edge

1/2"

First Fold

Apron Front

Press under lining upper edge 1/2", then another 1/2", concealing apron front upper raw edge; edgestitch.

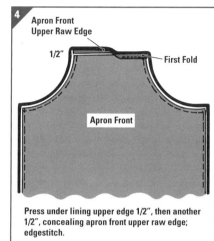

■ Encase the apron front/lining raw edges with bias binding from one armhole lower edge to the other armhole lower edge as shown in Figure 5, page 119.

■ Serge-finish the curved edges of the armhole facings. Right sides together, stitch one facing to each armhole area on the apron front, with the facing extending ½" beyond the upper and lower armhole edges; trim the seam to ¼" and clip the curves (Figure 6, page 119).

■ Press the facing to the apron lining side, turning under each

— **KID-BITS** —

The embroidered, long-skirted christening gown was developed in the 18th century, at which time a baby to be baptized also wore an embroidered cap and expensive colored mantle (a loose, sleeveless cloak-like garment worn over another garment).

5

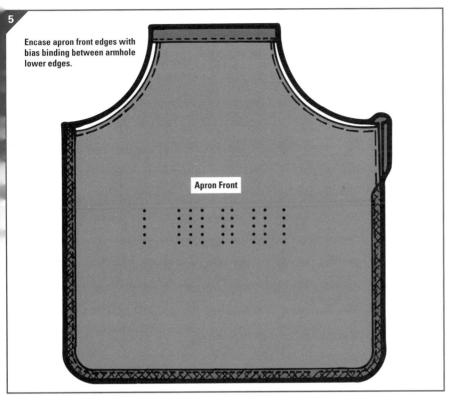

Encase apron front edges with bias binding between armhole lower edges.

Apron Front

side out, turning in the opening edges, and press; edge-stitch along both long edges.

■ Position the tool strap on the apron front, matching the tool strap stitching lines to the apron front stitching lines; stitch twice along each stitching line for reinforcement, backstitching securely at each end of each line, creating the tool sections.

Note: Depending on the tool sizes you plan to use, you may need to respace the stitching lines. The easiest way to do this is to stitch one strap end in place; position the tool as desired, pin-fitting the strap over it; mark with an air- or water-soluble marker; remove the tool; stitch twice along the marking as instructed above; and repeat with each tool until you reach the strap end.

6

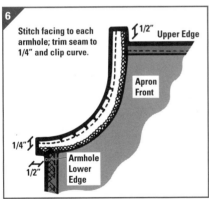

Stitch facing to each armhole; trim seam to 1/4" and clip curve.

1/2" Upper Edge

Apron Front

1/4"

Armhole Lower Edge

1/2"

7

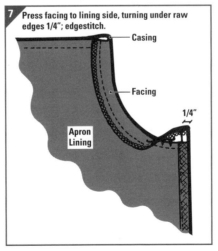

Press facing to lining side, turning under raw edges 1/4"; edgestitch.

Casing

Facing

Apron Lining

1/4"

raw edge ¼"; edgestitch in place, creating a casing (Figure 7).

■ Fold the tool strap in half lengthwise, right sides together; stitch along the strap raw

edges in a ¼" seam, leaving a 3" opening in the long edge for turning. Turn the strap right

■ Beginning at one armhole lower edge, thread the cording or ribbon through one armhole casing, then down through the other armhole casing, creating an adjustable neck cord and back ties; knot the ends (Figure 8). ❏

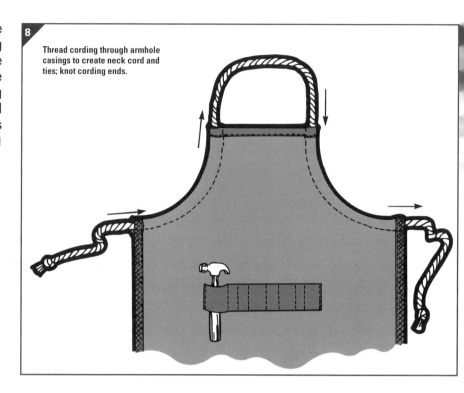

8

Thread cording through armhole casings to create neck cord and ties; knot cording ends.

— STAIN STRATEGIES —

It's disheartening to think your child has ruined a garment or other item you've sewn because of a stain, but we all know that dribbles and spills are common among little ones and difficult to avoid.

If you know the stain's origin, you have a head start at removing it. A stain from an unknown source, however, presents problems—treating it incorrectly could make the stain impossible to remove.

Follow these guidelines for conquering an unknown stain on washable fabrics:

■ Treat the stain as soon as possible. The longer a stain remains on the fabric, the more difficult it is to remove.

■ Treat the stain before machine drying or pressing the item, which can heat-set a stain.

■ Use the gentle pretreatment methods listed below, following the manufacturer's instructions for each stain-removal product.

• Soak the stain in cold water for 30 minutes. Rub detergent into the stain, wait 30 minutes, then rinse with cold water.

• Wash in warm water with detergent and bleach that is safe for the fabric. Allow the item to air dry.

• Apply a prewash stain remover.

• Use a presoak enzyme product.

• Wash with detergent in the hottest water that's safe for the fabric. Allow the item to air dry.

If the stain persists, consult a professional dry cleaner. ❏

for photo
finished project
on page 19

serger kids

Children are curious about everything, including the seemingly magical machine that creates—the serger. With its many spools of colorful thread, open-and-close doors and quick-as-a-flash way of creating fun clothes for kids, the serger is the closest thing to magic a little one may ever find!

If your child takes an interest in your serger, seize the opportunity to teach him a skill he may use for a lifetime. Children as young as 4 years old have enough dexterity to learn the basics, and slightly older children can actually learn to serge on their own. Young people are the ideal serger learners because they have no preconceived notions about how a serger should work, for example, why it would appear impossible to serge without fabric!

GETTING ACQUAINTED

To introduce your child to the serger, try the following simple orientation:

■ Explain serger safety rules, emphasizing the importance of keeping hands away from the needle and knife areas.

■ While allowing the child to watch, operate the serger without fabric.

■ Remove the thread from the machine and allow the child to sit at and operate the machine while you watch. The lack of thread will lessen the seemingly complicated nature of the machine, while eliminating the chance of thread problems that could lead to early frustration.

Note: If your child's legs are too short to reach the machine's foot pedal or if he is too young to control the serger's speed, let him sit on your lap while you control the foot pedal.

■ Allow children old enough to operate the serger without assistance to experiment with how much pressure to apply to the pedal and view the knives in action to see how they move in relation to each other.

■ When the child is completely comfortable with the machine, allow him to put fabric through the still-unthreaded machine to demonstrate the cutting process. This will familiarize the child with how much fabric can be cut off during actual use. Unbleached muslin works well for this task because it's inexpensive and creates little mess.

THREADING

■ Turn the serger's power off to avoid an accident.

■ Show the child the correct use of the tweezers and other accessories used to facilitate the threading process.

■ To help the child identify each thread's function and how the threads work together, color-code the threads to the machine's dials. *Note:* If your machine's dials aren't color-coded, add a piece of color-coded tape to each dial.

■ Using the diagram inside the serger's door, thread the first looper, proceeding logically and slowly. Remove the thread, set the tension dials at 0 and have the child rethread it, coaching him where necessary.

■ Using the same procedure, repeat with the second looper and needle thread(s).

PRACTICE MAKES PERFECT

■ Once the machine is threaded, let the child practice manipulating the fabric under the presser foot, serging on and off the fabric and controlling the fabric to ensure proper cutting.

■ Teach the child to raise the presser foot on the serger to begin a seam. This will prevent layers from slipping and serve as advance training for the conventional machine.

TENSION ADJUSTMENT

If the child is completely confident about the threading and simple straight sewing on the machine, consider introducing stitch length adjustment, basing your decision on your child's age, ability and attention span.

LET'S SERGE

For your child's first project, select a simple garment featuring straight seams and few pattern pieces. Guide your child toward fabrics appropriate to the pattern, especially those with a definite right side to help avoid confusion during construction. Do let him choose the pattern and fabric, counseling accordingly to build extra interest into the project.

PREPARATION

■ Preshrink the fabric, explaining to the child the importance of this step.

■ Separate and press the pattern pieces so the child can achieve quicker results.

■ If possible, have the child use pattern weights instead of pins for a speedy method of securing the pattern to the fabric.

■ To add fun to the cutting process (if your child has the skills), use a rotary cutter instead of shears. To demonstrate how it works, cut all the curved areas, leaving the easier, straight cuts for the child.

■ Show the child how to make shallow slashes to mark each notch, using tiny, easy-to-handle embroidery scissors.

■ Have the child practice serging a ⅝" seam on fabric scraps, so he can see how much fabric is trimmed. If the serger doesn't have a guide for a ⅝" seam, tape a clearly visible one on the front of the machine.

■ Use pins to match pattern pieces, but place them well outside the seam allowance, explaining to the child that serging over a pin can ruin the serger's knives or otherwise damage the machine.

CONSTRUCTION

The following sweatshirt sewing order allows almost complete in-the-flat construction, perfect for the novice fashion-sewer whose sewing skill may not be up to maneuvering curves and circles. The order is based on any simple sweatshirt pattern. *Note:*

Eliminate any pockets to streamline construction.

Practice making the garment yourself before expecting your child to do it. You'll find it easier to determine what he is capable of and anticipate questions.

Throughout the following instructions, advise the child as indicated, showing him the accompanying illustrations and letting him do as much of the actual construction as possible.

NECKLINE

■ Have the child serge the front and back pieces together at the shoulders in a ⅝" seam (Figure 1).

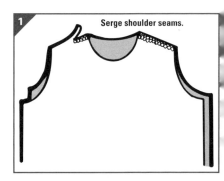

1 Serge shoulder seams.

■ On a conventional sewing machine, have the child seam the neckline ribbing ends in a ⅝" seam, forming a circle. Press the seam open for less bulk and easier attachment (Figure 2, page 123). Fold the ribbing in half lengthwise, wrong sides together, with raw edges matching.

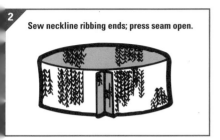

Sew neckline ribbing ends; press seam open.

■ Applying the neckline ribbing will be the most difficult step in the sweatshirt construction. To avoid discouragement, it's important to make its application as painless as possible:

• Help the child mark the shirt neckline and neckline ribbing in eighths, using two different colors of chalk or water-soluble markers, alternating every other color for each one-eighth mark and starting with the same color on the shirt and the ribbing (Figure 3).

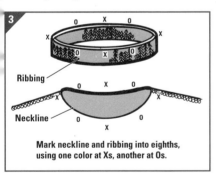

Mark neckline and ribbing into eighths, using one color at Xs, another at Os.

■ Position the ribbing and sweatshirt right sides together, with the ribbing seam at the sweatshirt center back. As the child serges, show him how to stretch the ribbing in a small area to match the colored mark on the ribbing with the corresponding mark on the neckline.

■ Once he understands, let the child serge around the remainder of the neckline edge, stopping just before reaching the beginning point.

■ Complete the neckline, showing the child how to serge overlapping stitches and serge off the seam.

CUFFS

■ Using the two-color marking technique explained for the neckline above, have the child divide each sleeve lower edge and cuff ribbing into quarters (Figure 4).

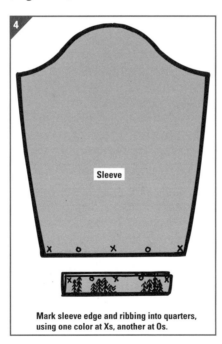

Sleeve

Mark sleeve edge and ribbing into quarters, using one color at Xs, another at Os.

■ Have the child repeat the above stretch-and-serge technique to apply the folded ribbing to the sleeves.

SLEEVES/SIDES

■ Help the child match the front and back sleeve clips to one sleeve cap, right sides together; pin, then serge the sleeve in place. Repeat for the other sleeve (Figure 5).

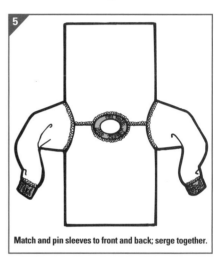

Match and pin sleeves to front and back; serge together.

■ Help the child match and pin one side/sleeve underarm seam from the hem to the wrist, right sides together; have him serge this seam continuously, leaving long thread tails at the seam beginning and end (Figure 6). *Note:* Leave the second side/sleeve underarm seam unserged until the waistline ribbing has been applied.

Serge side/sleeve underarm seam continuously, leaving thread tails.

■ Using the two-color marking technique explained for the neckline above, have the child divide the waistband ribbing and shirt lower edge into eighths.

■ Have the child repeat the above stretch-and-serge technique to apply the ribbing to the shirt lower edge (Figure 7).

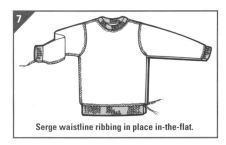

Serge waistline ribbing in place in-the-flat.

■ Have the child match, pin and serge the remaining side/sleeve underarm seam in the same manner as the first, serging through the cuff and waistband ribbing.

■ Show the child how to tuck the thread tail chains under the seam stitches using a tapestry needle (Figure 8).

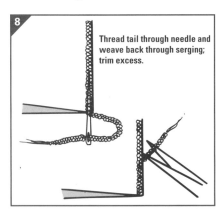

Thread tail through needle and weave back through serging; trim excess.

EMBELLISH

Help the child personalize the sweatshirt to his or her own style with simple adornments, such as the following:

■ Satin bows stitched to the sweatshirt front.

■ Machine-sewn lettering indicating the child's name, initials or favorite sports team on the sweatshirt front or down one sleeve.

■ Fusible appliqués outlined and embellished with fabric paints on the sweatshirt front.

❑

— THE LONG & SHORT OF IT —

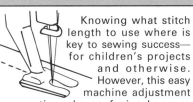

Knowing what stitch length to use where is key to sewing success—for children's projects and otherwise. However, this easy machine adjustment can sometimes be confusing because stitch length is measured in two ways: stitches per inch and length of stitch.

When measured in *stitches per inch*, the range is usually from 6 to 20, plus fine or 0. The *higher* the number, the *shorter* the stitch.

When measured by *length of stitch*, the range is usually from 0 to 4, 5 or 6. These numbers represent the length of each stitch measured in millimeters, so the *higher* the number, the *longer* the stitch.

To determine stitch length, consider fabric type and sewing technique. The normal stitch length for general-purpose sewing, including seams, is 10 to 12 stitches per inch or 2mm to 2.5mm. As a general guide for other types of sewing refer to the accompanying chart.

In addition:
■ Use a longer stitch for heavyweight fabrics, dense or tightly woven fabrics or when sewing leather, vinyl or plastic to avoid ripping along the seamline.
■ Use a shorter stitch for lightweight fabrics and lace, curved seams or seams on the bias.

❑

STITCH EQUIVALENTS & USES

STITCH LENGTH (MM)	STITCHES PER INCH	STITCH USES
0	0	STITCHING IN PLACE
0.25	100	
0.5	50	SATIN STITCHING
1	25	
1.25	20	REINFORCEMENT STITCHING
1.5	16	
2	12	GENERAL-PURPOSE STITCHING
2.5	10	
3	8	TOPSTITCHING, EASESTITCHING, GATHERING
4	6	
5	5	
6	4	BASTING

ART TO WEAR

Give your child an art start—wearable art, that is! Appliqué, colorblocking, creative serging, button art. These are just a few of the many ways you can embellish clothing to make a creative, lively statement on children's clothing and accessories.

Like wearable art for adults, kids' wearable art warrants certain design guidelines and considerations, such as: Are appliqué motif shapes and sizes compatible with that of the silhouette? Does the design element suit the intended wearer's taste and personality? Are the chosen fabrics, notions and other embellishments care-compatible? Have you placed the adornments in locations to complement the wearer's best features and maybe even tickle his or her fancy? Do the colors work together in a pleasing manner to complement the overall design?

Ask yourself these questions *before* beginning to cut and sew to ensure the greatest success. And do trial layouts or even sew small, rough prototypes before beginning—you'll often find ways to make a design even better after seeing it assembled. Changes might involve using additional trims, making the design more elaborate or streamlining and simplifying for a cleaner, less-cluttered look.

The following stories detail some whimsical wearable art garments, ensembles and accents that will make kids squeal with delight.

"Catching Some Gs" (cover garment) makes a bold, friendly statement, using appliqué and a bit of creative serging to finish the appliqué outer edges before application. A fringe mane and forelock, twitching ears and wiggle eyes give him the three-dimensional appeal children adore.

Color-blocking is the simple technique explained in "Workout Wow!", featuring complete instructions for creating a color-blocked leotard for your little gymnast. We fabricated it in four coordinating Lycra®-based fabrics—one print and three solids pulled from the print—for a colorful, artistic piece. The story also features inspiration and instructions for making other workout extras.

And "Cute As A Button" focuses on fanciful button art, with two simple-to-make accessories—button-embellished tennies and suspenders—even kids can fashion with just a bit of adult supervision.

These are just a few of your options for making art to wear. Let our sample projects and instructions inspire you, then use your imagination and creativity to make items for your child to wear with flair. ❏

or photo
nished project
on page 21

catching some gs

The "Gs" have it! Giraffes that is! Your preschooler or kindergartner will surely love this "skimp outfit" with its imaginative giraffe appliqué. The simple shapes make this an easy-to-sew project for back-to-school or just for fun. You can use your serger and decorative thread to add emphasis to the larger shapes, if you wish, or apply all the shapes with satin stitching. Then pop the embellished oversized top over spotted leggings to complete the look.

MATERIALS

• Any basic sweatshirt pattern, featuring the following: long, set-in sleeves; ribbed cuffs, neckline and lower edge; and one-piece front and back

• Any leggings-type pant pattern

• Red and white spotted or dotted interlock knit for leggings as specified on the pattern envelope, plus ½ yard

• Red interlock knit and white ribbing for top as specified on the pattern envelope

• ¼ yard of white lightweight broadcloth or poplin

• ¾ yard of black 1"-wide cotton upholstery fringe

• One set of "wiggle eye" buttons or safety eyes

• Two ¼"-diameter black buttons for nostrils

• 9" x 20" rectangle of white lightweight woven interfacing

• ½ yard of fusible transfer web

• Scraps of polyester fiberfill

• Two spools of all-purpose and one spool of decorative black thread if serge-finishing appliqués, or two spools of all-purpose black thread if satin stitching appliqués

• Water-soluble marker

• Pattern tracing cloth

CONSTRUCTION

■ Preshrink all fabric, trim and interfacing.

■ Cut and construct the leggings following the pattern guidesheet.

■ Lengthen the top front and back pattern pieces 2" (1" on sizes smaller than 4), then cut the front, back and sleeves from the red knit.

■ On the adjusted top front pattern piece, sketch in the giraffe body pattern, making it 4" tall at the center front and curving down to 1½" at the side seams (Figure 1). *Note:* For sizes smaller than 4, the body pattern should measure 3" at the center front and 1" at the side seams.

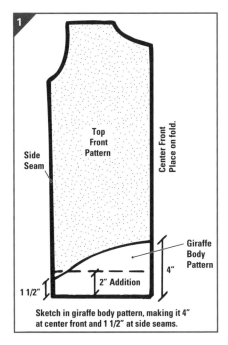

1

Sketch in giraffe body pattern, making it 4" at center front and 1 1/2" at side seams.

■ Cut one giraffe body from the red and white spotted knit and one from interfacing.

■ Enlarge the pattern pieces in Figure 2.

■ From the red and white spotted knit, cut one head, one tail and one 3"x11" rectangle for the neck. Cut one neck and one tail from the interfacing.

■ From the white broadcloth, cut four ears.

■ Apply fusible web to the remaining white broadcloth wrong side; cut two horns from this fabric.

■ Using a water-soluble marker, transfer the placement markings to the right side of the head and two of the ears as indicated on the patterns.

■ Glue or machine baste the interfacing to the body, tail and neck wrong side.

■ If you have access to a serger, finish the following with black decorative thread, such as topstitching thread in the upper looper, using a balanced tension and a wide, closely spaced stitch: the body upper curved edge; the head; the tail upper and side edges; and the 11" neck edges (Figure 3). I not, apply fusible transfer web to the wrong side of each piece and leave the edges unstitched for now.

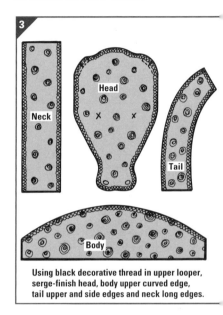

Using black decorative thread in upper looper, serge-finish head, body upper curved edge, tail upper and side edges and neck long edges.

■ Baste a strip of the upholstery fringe under the tail upper edge, pushing the tufts closely together (Figure 4).

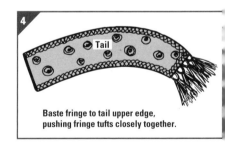

Baste fringe to tail upper edge, pushing fringe tufts closely together.

■ Baste a strip of the upholstery fringe under one long neck edge, pushing the tufts closely together to create a mane (Figure 5, page 129).

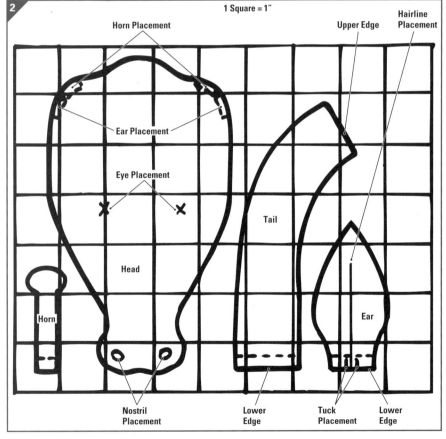

1 Square = 1"

Horn Placement

Upper Edge

Hairline Placement

Ear Placement

Eye Placement

Tail

Head

Horn

Ear

Nostril Placement

Lower Edge

Tuck Placement

Lower Edge

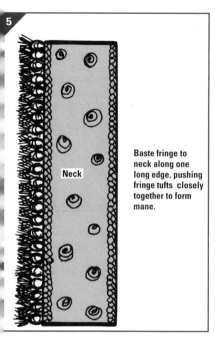

5

Baste fringe to neck along one long edge, pushing fringe tufts closely together to form mane.

Neck

■ Using a closely spaced zigzag and black thread, stitch the hairline on two ears, following the placement markings.

■ Right sides together and using a ¼" seam allowance, stitch one satin stitched ear to one plain ear, leaving the lower edge open; repeat with the remaining ears. Trim the seams, turn each ear right side out and press. Stuff each ear lightly with polyester fiberfill, then straight stitch down the center of each ear's satin stitched hairline to achieve a subtle quilted effect.

■ Following the placement markings, make a tuck at each ear lower raw edge; baste in place.

■ With the satin stitched sides facing up, pin the ears to the head upper edge, overlapping each ear lower edge ¼" (Figure 6).

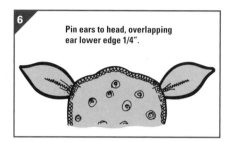

6

Pin ears to head, overlapping ear lower edge 1/4".

■ Machine baste the body, tail and neck to the top front, with the tail approximately 2" from the side seam and the neck approximately ½" from the tail, tucking the tail and neck lower edge under the body upper edge; pin the head in place, positioning it at a slight angle, with the head upper edge about 2" from the top neckline and overlapping the giraffe neck upper edge (Figure 7).

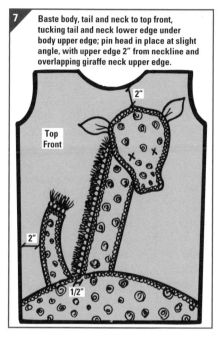

7

Baste body, tail and neck to top front, tucking tail and neck lower edge under body upper edge; pin head in place at slight angle, with upper edge 2" from neckline and overlapping giraffe neck upper edge.

2"

Top Front

2"

1/2"

— DON'T MAKE WAVES! —

If you like narrow, topstitched hems on children's clothing, but avoid them because stitching ripples and waves often accompany this technique on flared or circular skirts, calm the waves with interfacing! Use a ¾"-wide strip of lightweight fusible tricot interfacing cut on the bias to easily shape to the curve of the hem and give with the fabric.
■ Mark the hem foldline.
■ Trim the hem allowance to 1".
■ Position the interfacing on the hem allowance wrong side, with the interfacing lower edge even with the hem foldline; fuse in place, following the manufacturer's instructions.
■ Finish the hem raw edge in a manner appropriate for the fabric.
■ Fold the hem allowance to the wrong side along the hem foldline; pin at right angles to the fold.

■ On the fabric right side, topstitch ⅝" from the folded edge (Figure 1).

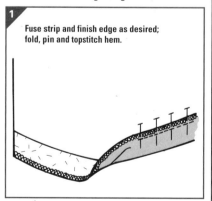

1

Fuse strip and finish edge as desired; fold, pin and topstitch hem.

This ripple-banishing technique will also add body and improve the drape and hang of the hem. ❏

■ If you serged the body, tail and neck edges, topstitch these pieces in place close to the outer edge of each. If the pieces weren't serge-finished, remove the fusible web paper backing and fuse the body and tail in place, then stitch around the edges with a wide, closely spaced satin stitch, using black thread.

■ Center and tuck a strip of the upholstery fringe under the head upper edge between the horn placement markings for the forelock; pin. Position a horn on each side of the fringe, following the placement markings and tucking the straight edge of each under the head ¼". Fuse each horn in place, then satin stitch around the edge of each using black thread.

■ If you serged around the head, topstitch it in place close to the head outer edge. If it wasn't serge-finished, remove the fusible web paper backing and fuse the head in place, then satin stitch around the edges with black thread.

■ Sew the "wiggle eye" buttons on the head for eyes and the black buttons on the head for nostrils, following the placement markings (Figure 8).

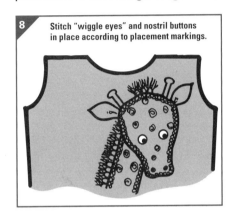

8 Stitch "wiggle eyes" and nostril buttons in place according to placement markings.

■ Complete the top following the pattern guidesheet. ❑

— ZIP TIPS —

The following hints will help your kids use the zippers on their clothing and accessories without a hitch:

■ If the zipper doesn't slide smoothly, rub the teeth with pencil lead or spray it with a no-stick cooking spray, such as Pam®, taking care to protect the project fabric from either item.

■ If a metal zipper won't remain zipped while the garment is being worn, give it a good shot of hair spray, being careful to protect the garment fabric while spraying.

■ Avoid the "blip" (wide spot) when stitching around the zipper pull by using a zipper longer than the pattern suggests for the placket opening, then complete the zipper stitching, unzip the zipper and cut off the excess length.

■ Help children dress themselves by adding ribbons or decorative baubles to the zipper pull, making the pull easier for small hands to maneuver.

■ To reuse a zipper from a discarded garment, remove it, then spray it with starch to renew its stable hand. ❑

or photo
nished projects
on page 20

bloomin' bloomers

Give your baby girl's toddler wardrobe a touch of sugar and spice with eyelet-trimmed bloomers. Sewing them yourself lets you unleash your creativity to capture your little darling's personality—and saves you most of the $20-plus these undies garner at upscale children's boutiques.

To create the focal point of these pretty panties, embellish the rear view using the appliqué patterns provided or create your own to suit your tot's fancy. The pattern given is a toddler's size 2 or 3, designed to fit nicely over a young tot's diapers or to be worn as underwear by an average-sized 2- to 3-year-old. To increase the pattern size, add 1/4" to the pattern pieces' perimeters for *each* size larger.

MATERIALS

• ½ yard of 45"-wide cotton broadcloth, chambray or mini-print fabric for panty body

• 1 yard of ¾"- to 1"-wide flat white eyelet lace trim

• ⅜ yard of ⅜"-wide satin or grosgrain ribbon

• 1 yard of ¼"-wide white elastic

• 1 yard of ½"-wide single-fold bias tape to match panty or appliqué fabric

• Small amounts of appliqué fabrics of your choice

• ¼ yard of lightweight fusible interfacing

• ¼ yard of fusible transfer web

• ¼ yard of tear-away stabilizer

• Air-soluble marker

• ⅔ yard of narrow rickrack or piping or ¾"-wide eyelet for trimming back seams (optional)

• 5" of ⅛"-wide green satin ribbon (for "Cherries Jubilee" panties only)

• Matching thread

PREPARATION/CUTTING

■ Enlarge the panty body patterns and the desired appliqué patterns in Figure 1, page 132, or enlarge the panty body patterns only and use your own appliqué patterns to fit the area. *Note:* Panty body patterns include ¼" seam allowances, unless otherwise indicated; appliqué patterns include *no* seam allowances unless otherwise indicated.

■ Preshrink and press the fabric and trim(s). Cut the panty pieces from the panty body fabric, then set the front/sides and back lining pieces aside.

EMBELLISHMENT

■ Back the appliqué fabrics with fusible interfacing, then fusible transfer web, following the manufacturer's instructions for each.

■ Cut out the appliqués from the desired fabrics. Using the air-soluble marker, draw in any details to be highlighted by stitching on the appliqué right sides.

■ *For the "Cherries Jubilee" panties* (refer to the photo on page 20 for placement guidelines):

• Right sides together, stitch around each set of leaves, leaving an opening for turning as indicated on the pattern.

• Clip the corners, turn the leaves right side out and slipstitch the openings closed.

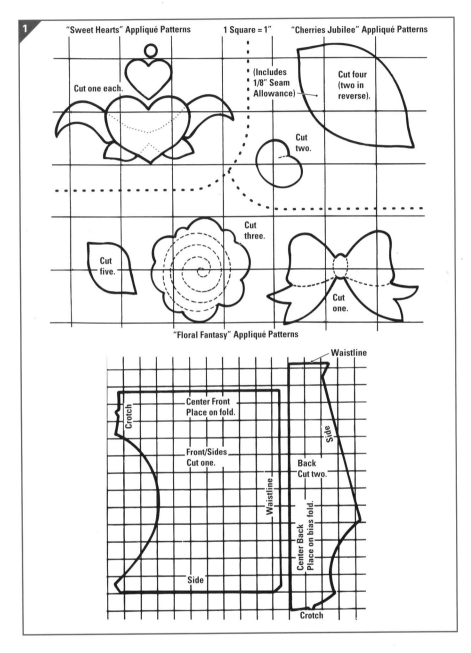

1

"Sweet Hearts" Appliqué Patterns   1 Square = 1"   "Cherries Jubilee" Appliqué Patterns

Cut one each.

(Includes 1/8" Seam Allowance)

Cut four (two in reverse).

Cut two.

Cut three.

Cut five.

Cut one.

"Floral Fantasy" Appliqué Patterns

Waistline

Crotch

Center Front Place on fold.

Side

Front/Sides Cut one.

Back Cut two.

Waistline

Center Back Place on bias fold.

Side

Crotch

• Pinch each leaf base to form a tiny pleat and topstitch as shown (Figure 2).

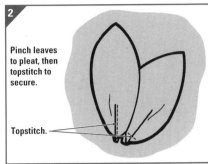

2

Pinch leaves to pleat, then topstitch to secure.

Topstitch.

• Fold the green satin ribbon in half at an approximately 45 degree angle and topstitch in place for cherry stems.

■ Using the photo on page 2(as a guide, position and fuse the appliqués in place. *Note* For the "Cherries Jubilee" panties, fuse the cherries in place over the ends of the ribbon stems.

■ Cut a piece of tear-away stabilizer larger than the entire appliqué area and pin or baste it inside the panty behind the appliqué area.

■ Using a narrow, dense zigzag stitch and matching thread, stitch along all appliqué edges, allowing the needle swing to span the edges *Note:* Practice on scraps to determine the best stitch

Using the same zigzag, stitch over any internal appliqué markings.

■ Trim away the excess stabilizer and press the appliqué area.

■ To trim the back seams with rickrack, piping or eyelet, baste the desired trim close to the side edges, right sides together.

PANTY CONSTRUCTION

Note: Use ¼" seam allowances unless otherwise indicated.

■ Place the back and back lining right sides together, with raw edges even, then sandwich the front/sides in between, with the raw edges of one side edge even; stitch the side seam, beginning at the base of the corner angle as shown in Figure 3. Press the back lining away from the front/sides.

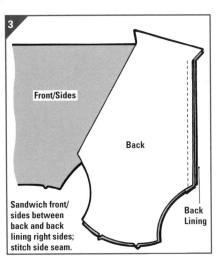

Sandwich front/sides between back and back lining right sides; stitch side seam.

■ Right sides together, stitch the remaining side of the back to the remaining side of the front/sides, beginning at the base of the corner angle; press both side seams toward the back.

■ Press under ¼" on the remaining back lining side and baste in place over the second seam, beginning ½" below the waistline edge. Topstitch ⅛" in from both seams along the basting (Figure 4); remove the basting.

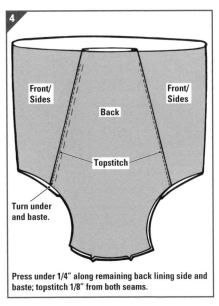

Press under 1/4" along remaining back lining side and baste; topstitch 1/8" from both seams.

■ To make the waistline casing, press under the waistline edge of the front/sides ⅛", then ⅜", and pin in place. Stitch close to the first fold, *leaving the back unstitched* (Figure 5).

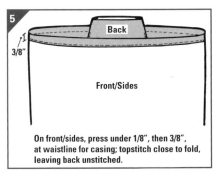

On front/sides, press under 1/8", then 3/8", at waistline for casing; topstitch close to fold, leaving back unstitched.

■ Cut a 14" length of elastic (½" longer for each size larger) and insert it into the casing using a small safety pin. With the panties right side out, fold down the waistline extension on the back only. Allowing the elastic to extend slightly beyond the front/sides edges, stitch and backstitch over the elastic ends on the back lining only (Figure 6).

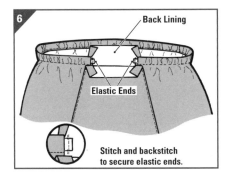

Stitch and backstitch to secure elastic ends.

■ Press under the back and back lining waistline edge ¼", then ⅜", encasing the elastic ends. Baste close to the first fold, then topstitch a rectangle close to all edges of the back waistline (Figure 7, page 134). Remove the basting.

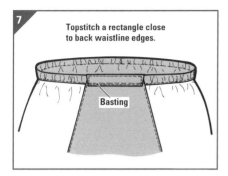

7 Topstitch a rectangle close to back waistline edges.

Basting

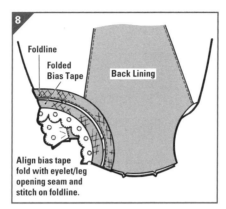

8 Foldline

Folded Bias Tape

Back Lining

Align bias tape fold with eyelet/leg opening seam and stitch on foldline.

■ Cut two lengths of eyelet trim the leg opening circumference, plus ½". Right sides together, stitch one length of trim to each leg opening; press the seam allowances toward the panty.

■ To add a bias tape casing to each leg opening:

• Unfold one edge of the bias tape; pin the bias tape with the exposed fold even with the leg/eyelet seam on the panty wrong side and the larger portion of the bias tape width extending away from the panty, then stitch along the exposed bias tape fold (Figure 8); trim the excess bias tape at the ends.

• Fold in the bias tape smoothly to form a casing; pin and topstitch close to the remaining fold (Figure 9).

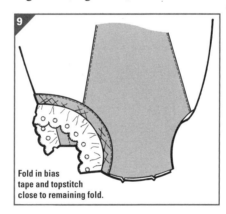

9

Fold in bias tape and topstitch close to remaining fold.

■ Cut two 11" elastic lengths (add ½" for each size larger). Using a small safety pin, insert the elastic into the leg opening casings; tack each elastic end to secure.

■ *Wrong* sides together, pin the front/sides to the back at the crotch and stitch in a ⅛" seam, catching the elastic ends. Turn the panty wrong side out; stitch the crotch seam again in a ¼" seam to form a French seam (Figure 10).

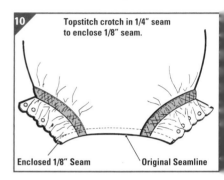

10 Topstitch crotch in 1/4" seam to enclose 1/8" seam.

Enclosed 1/8" Seam   Original Seamline

■ Cut the ⅜"-wide ribbon in half, tie two bows and tack one at each back seam over the leg casing. ❑

bow-dacious

Delight the little darling in your life with this glamour-girl velour pant set. She'll love the satin-bow-trimmed top and jazzy pull-on pants with ruffle embellishment. The sewing is easy and yardage minimal, allowing you to make it quickly for about one-half the ready-to-wear price.

MATERIALS

• Any pull-on, long-sleeved, sweatshirt-styled top and pull-on pant pattern in your child's size

• 60"-wide velour in the yardage specified on the pattern envelope, plus ½ yard

• Matching rib knit trim in the yardage specified on the pattern envelope

• Washable (hand or machine) polyester satin in three different colors. Purchase ¼ yard of each or search your scrap box—you'll need a 5½" X 9" rectangle of each color.

• Small scrap of fusible weft-insertion interfacing

• Pattern tracing cloth

CUTTING

■ Using the top pattern pieces, draft a neckline facing pattern for the top front and back: Measure down 2" from the neckline at the center front on the pattern tissue and draw a line that curves up to mid-shoulder (Figure 1); repeat on the back pattern piece. Trace the facing onto pattern tracing cloth.

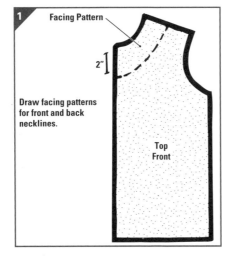

Following the adjusted layout (Figure 2), cut the top, facings, pants and 4"-wide leg ruffle strips from the velour; determine the ruffle strips' length by measuring the pant pattern side seam and multiplying by 1.5.

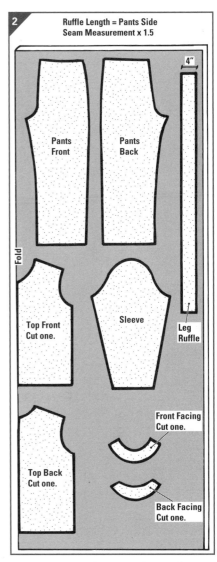

■ Cut each facing from interfacing.

■ Cut a 4" x 6" rectangle and 1½" x 9" strip from each color of satin for the bows.

■ Cut the leg cuff, sleeve cuff and top lower edge bands from the rib knit. *Note:* Do not cut a neckband from the ribbing; a facing replaces the neckband.

PANTS CONSTRUCTION

■ Fold each ruffle in half lengthwise, right sides together, and stitch the short ends in a gentle curve, beginning at the raw edge and curving in to the fold (Figure 3). Trim the seam, turn and press carefully.

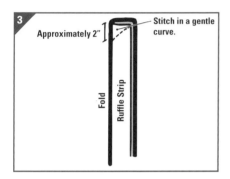

Figure 3: Approximately 2" — Stitch in a gentle curve. Fold — Ruffle Strip

■ Easestitch the ruffle raw edge through both layers, stitching ⅜" and ⅝" from the edge.

■ Raw edges matching, pin each ruffle to the side seam of one front pant leg right side, placing one end ⅝" from the pant leg lower edge, the other end 2½" from the upper edge (Figure 4). Draw up the gathers to fit, distributing the gathers evenly; stitch.

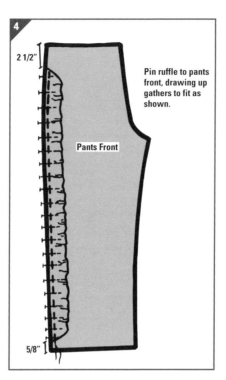

Figure 4: 2 1/2" — Pin ruffle to pants front, drawing up gathers to fit as shown. Pants Front — 5/8"

■ Complete the pants following the pattern guidesheet.

TOP CONSTRUCTION

■ Staystitch the front and back neckline. Set aside.

■ Fold one satin rectangle in half crosswise, right sides together. Stitch the raw edges together using ¼" seam allowances and short stitches, leaving an opening on one side for turning (Figure 5). Clip the corners, turn the piece right side out and press; slipstitch the opening closed. Repeat with the remaining satin rectangles.

■ Easestitch the center of each completed satin rectangle and draw up to a width of 1" to

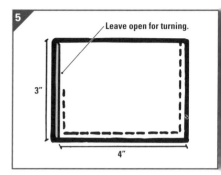

Figure 5: Leave open for turning. 3" — 4"

form a bow (Figure 6). Knot the thread ends to secure the gathering and set aside.

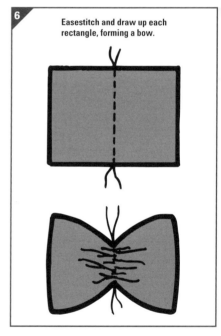

Figure 6: Easestitch and draw up each rectangle, forming a bow.

■ Fold each 9" satin strip in half lengthwise, right sides together, and stitch in a ¼" seam. Turn right side out and press.

■ Fold one end of each finished strip around the corresponding-colored bow and stitch to secure (Figure 7, page 137).

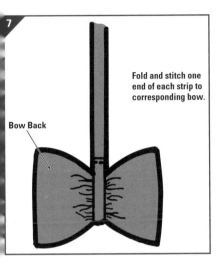

Fold and stitch one end of each strip to corresponding bow.

Bow Back

■ Center and pin one bow/strip on the top front right side so the bow is positioned 2" to 3" below the armhole seamline. Edgestitch along the strip's long edges, continuing through the bow (Figure 8).

■ Position the remaining bows so they extend from the neckline at the shoulder to 1" above the already-applied bow. Pin and stitch in place as indicated above, trimming the strips even with the neckline edge (Figure 9).

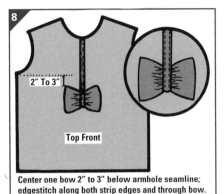

2" To 3"

Top Front

Center one bow 2" to 3" below armhole seamline; edgestitch along both strip edges and through bow.

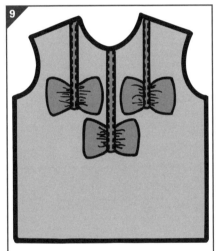

Stitch remaining bows in place with strips extending from neckline/shoulder intersection.

■ Complete the top following the pattern guidesheet, disregarding the neckband instructions.

■ Fuse the interfacing to the corresponding facing pieces. Right sides together, stitch the facing shoulder seams; trim the seams to ¼" and press them open. Serge-finish or pink and edgestitch the facing lower edge.

■ Right sides together, stitch the facing to the neckline. Trim and grade the seam, turn the facing to the top wrong side and press. Topstitch the neckline ¼" from the finished edge, breaking the stitching at the satin strips (Figure 10).

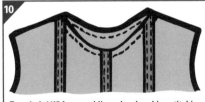

Topstitch 1/4" from neckline edge, breaking stitching at satin strips.

Color photo of finished project on page 21

workout wow!

Sewing exercisewear for kids is a natural—after all, who indulges in more physical activity than a child? Children love the bright and splashy Lycra® blends shown in today's aerobicwear, not to mention their wearing ease and comfort, and mothers will appreciate the easy-sew nature and minimal materials required to sew leotards.

FABRIC

Two-way stretch (often called four-way stretch) fabric is a requisite for sewing workoutwear, and the color and pattern choices grow more varied by the season. Refer to the stretch gauge on the pattern envelope to make sure your chosen fabric has enough stretch in both directions to accommodate the design.

Cotton/Lycra blends are a favorite among exercise nuts today, due to the great stretch for fit and ease of movement and the soft hand and wonderful absorbency for comfort. These blends often include a bit of polyester, too, to aid in abrasion-resistance and fabric strength—especially effective for childrenswear.

Nylon/Lycra is another popular combination, also offering great stretch for fit and ease of movement, as well as spectacular color saturation and a satiny sheen, due to nylon's great affinity for dyes. This combination also affords exceptional strength, but low absorbency qualities, so it tends to retain body heat.

Keep these points in mind when choosing leotard styles, opting for cotton/Lycra blends in long-sleeved varieties for optimum comfort and coolness, nylon/Lycra varieties for the boldest, most colorful results.

PATTERN DESIGNS

Although children are shaped differently than adults, basic body types exist in both child and adult figures: short, stocky, tall, bony, round, etc. Choose the style that best suits your child's build, keeping in mind children have an innate sense about the way they want to look. Proper choices *before* sewing can make the differ-ence between a much-worn item and one shunned by a self-conscious youngster.

Although you won't find an abundance of children's exercisewear patterns available, don't let that deter you. For optimum versatility, adapt swimsuit or skating patterns into leotard designs, making sure first, however, that the pattern specifies a built-in stretch factor of 100 percent in one direction, 50 to 100 percent in the other direction. Exercise or aerobic garb should be created to allow complete freedom of movement when worn for strenuous physical activities, so purchase patterns accordingly.

SEWING TIPS

■ Preshrink fabric to eliminate shrinkage later and remove excess fabric finishes that can cause skipped stitches.

■ Always use a "with-nap" pattern layout to avoid subtle or dramatic shading differences in finished garments.

■ When cutting, do not allow the fabric to hang over a surface edge, as the fabric's stretch may cause distortion.

■ Carefully follow the lengthwise grainline location; patterns will indicate positioning so the stretchiest part of the fabric goes around the body—often the lengthwise grain on actionwear fabrics.

■ Use fine ball point pins to avoid snagging the fabric, and use sharp shears or a rotary cutter for cutting.

■ Use a *new* No. 9 (size 70) or No. 11 (size 80) ball point needle and polyester/cotton thread. Blunt or bent needles will snag the fabric and cause skipped stitches.

■ Before stitching permanently, check the fit on the child by basting the garment together first.

■ Because exercisewear seams need to be resilient, a serged or overlocked seam is ideal, however your conventional machine's stretch stitch will also work well, and all of the above will allow you to skip extra seam finishes.

■ If you're limited to using a straight stitch, build in stretch as you stitch by holding the fabric tautly in front of and behind the presser foot, stretching gently, while stitching. Then stitch again within the seam allowances in the same manner and trim the seam allowances close to the second stitching. Make several test seams first to determine the best seam choice for your project.

■ If you need or want stability in some garment areas, such as the shoulder and waistline seams, stitch these seams with a straight stitch, then stabilize with narrow twill tape.

Create unique exercisewear by adding personalized pizzazz to each project. The following popular looks are simple to duplicate.

COLOR BLOCKING

Use an existing pattern and splice in a new color or color combination. Consider allowing the child to choose the colors and the arrangement to add excitement and involvement.

■ Select the pattern section suitable for color blocking, such as the front (vertically, horizontally, diagonally, etc.).

■ Trace this portion onto another piece of paper or tissue, keeping the original pattern intact. If the area you select is a piece normally cut on the fold, such as a front or back, trace one half, then flip it over and trace the mirror-image, so you can work with the entire piece.

■ On the newly traced pattern piece, draw the "design" lines; number the pieces and put notches between each section on the new lines and add a grainline to each piece to ensure proper stretch (Figure 1).

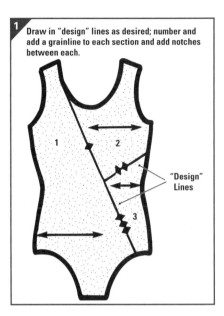

Draw in "design" lines as desired; number and add a grainline to each section and add notches between each.

"Design" Lines

■ Cut apart the sections and retrace each, adding ¼" seam allowances to each newly cut edge; transfer the notches to the new cutting lines (Figure 2).

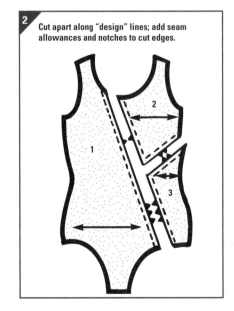

Cut apart along "design" lines; add seam allowances and notches to cut edges.

■ Cut your new pattern in the colors/designs desired, then piece it together as you assemble the garment, watching it come to life!

TWO-FROM-ONE!

Most leotard patterns have only two patterns pieces, front and back, and both are cut on the fold, or occasionally have a center seamline. Either of these styles may be converted into a two-piece leotard for fashion appeal.

■ For the bottoms, measure up from the pattern front and back crotch areas to the desired waistline location; draw a line at this location from side seam to side seam.

• Trace the bottoms areas onto paper or tissue, adding a ¼" seam allowance along the upper edges (Figure 3).

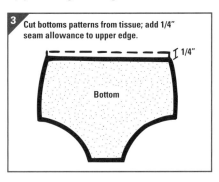

3 Cut bottoms patterns from tissue; add 1/4" seam allowance to upper edge.

↕ 1/4"

Bottom

• Cut a bottoms front and back from your fabric; right sides together, stitch the side seams, then turn the bottoms right side out.

• Measure the bottoms waistline and cut a waistband this length, plus ½" for seam allowances, and 2½" in width.

• Fold the waistband in half lengthwise, wrong sides together, with a waistband length of 1"-wide elastic sandwiched in between. Stitch the short edges together in a ¼" seam; press the seam open.

• Raw edges even, position the waistband along the leotard bottoms waistline edge; stitch the three cut edges (two waistband, one leotard) together in a ¼" seam, being careful not to catch the elastic (Figure 4).

• Right sides together, stitch the crotch seam.

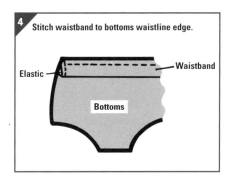

4 Stitch waistband to bottoms waistline edge.

Elastic — Waistband

Bottoms

■ For the top, trim the leotard front and back patterns to the desired length (midriff to hip length), plus a hem allowance, then cut one of each from your fabric and finish according to the pattern guidesheet, hemming the lower edge or adding an elastic casing.

OVER-SHORTS

A pair of over-shorts from the leotard fabric, a coordinate or a combination of several coordinates is a fun addition to any actionwear wardrobe.

■ Using a basic boxer shorts pattern with an elasticized waistline, cut the front and back from the same or different fabrics, color blocking as explained above, if desired (Figure 5).

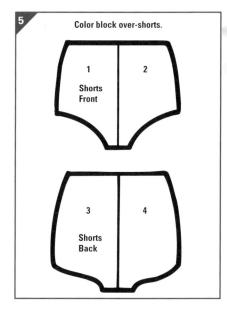

5 Color block over-shorts.

1 2

Shorts Front

3 4

Shorts Back

TRIANGULAR OVER-TOP

A snazzy way to dress up children's exercisewear is to make an over-top of a contrasting or coordinating solid or print.

■ Construct the leotard as desired.

■ Cut a modified triangular-shaped pattern using the following measurements: one shoulder measurement from the base of the neck to the shoulder tip (A); the desired length (B); one-half of the waist measurement, plus 16" (C) (Figure 6, page 141).

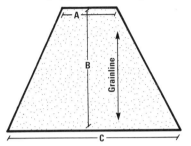

6 Cut pattern based on following measurements: one shoulder from base of neck to shoulder tip (A); desired length (B); one-half of waist, plus 16" (C).

A

B — Grainline

C

■ Cut two of this pattern from the desired fabric.

■ Stitch the shoulder seams together in a ¼" seam.

■ Finish all raw edges with a serger or narrow rolled hem and straight stitch.

■ Position the shoulder seam over one shoulder, then tie the ends at the waistline or hipline (Figure 7).

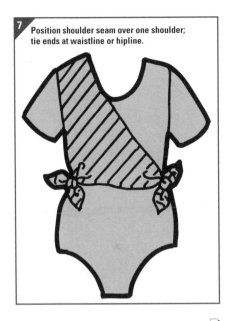

7 Position shoulder seam over one shoulder; tie ends at waistline or hipline.

— A PERFECT MATCH —

Plaids add an exciting, youthful and classic dimension to children's fashions and accessories, and matching the design results in professional-looking finished projects that are fun to wear and visually pleasing.

Plaids should flow around the body, matching at the side seams, center front, center back and front armhole notch. The design should also maintain a continuous vertical line from the garment upper edge to the garment lower edge.

When cutting out a plaid, position the most important pattern piece—the garment front—first. Always match *stitching* lines, not cutting lines.

When sewing, the following speedy basting tape technique results in perfectly matched seams every time, *even* with plaids cut on the bias!

■ Press under the seam allowance on one garment section.
■ Place basting tape ¹⁄₁₆" from the seam allowance fold on the pressed-under portion.
■ Peel the paper backing from the basting tape.
■ Position the folded seam allowance on top of the corresponding garment section, matching the design at the seamline (Figure 1).
■ From the garment wrong side, stitch the seam, using the folded creaseline as a guide.
■ Remove the basting tape *before* pressing.

Now your garment can be plaid-perfect—in record time!

1 Apply basting tape 1/16" from seam allowance fold; position garment section over corresponding garment sections.

Basting Tape

cute as a button

We all have them: assorted buttons in odd shapes, sizes and colors—the leftovers from projects past. You may have them in bags, jars or boxes. Or maybe they're a jumble at the bottom of your sewing basket. Though these little odds and ends may seem to have little worth when viewed separately, collectively they're worth their weight in gold! Just look at the be-buttoned tennies and suspenders on page 21 and you'll see what we mean. As embellishments for children's accessories, they gain new life in simple yet clever ways, and when combined with other trims and treasures—rickrack, laces, etc.—creative possibilities are virtually endless!

BUTTON RX

For children age 3 and under, it's wise to avoid the excessive use of buttons. Toddlers have strong, curious hands, and you don't want buttons turned into munchables!

To securely attach buttons to accessories for these little ones, use either elastic thread—this allows some stretch while also affording strength—or dental floss. However, use the latter on sturdy, tightly woven fabrics *only*; the floss is so strong, the fabric may tear before the button pulls off.

Launch your button adventure with a simple, quick accessory like those described below, then let your creativity roam and embellish sweatshirts, outerwear, hair accents—whatever suits your fancy.

MULTI-MOTIF SNEAKERS

MATERIALS

• One pair of white canvas slip-on tennis shoes

• Approximately 40 assorted primary-colored novelty buttons

• 1 yard of red mini rickrack

• White craft glue

• Red thread

• Masking tape

• Pliers or wire cutters

INSTRUCTIONS

■ Hand stitch the rickrack around the bias binding at the shoe opening, overlapping the ends at the shoe back (Figure 1).

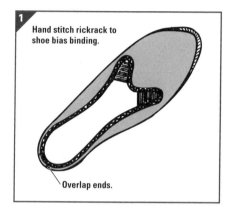

1
Hand stitch rickrack to shoe bias binding.

Overlap ends.

■ Using the pliers or wirecutters, snip off the backs of any shank buttons.

■ Divide the buttons into two equal groups—one for each shoe. Glue the buttons to the shoes as desired, using the photo on page 21 as a guide, if desired, and secure them with tape. Allow the glue to dry overnight, then remove the masking tape. Check each button for security and re-glue any not well-attached.

SPRIGHTLY SUSPENDERS

MATERIALS

• 1½ yards of 1"-wide solid-colored stretch belting

• Four heart-motif suspender clips

Two of each of the following buttons: A, B, C, large apple, gold star, pencil

Matching thread. *Note:* You will also need elastic thread or floss if the suspenders are for a child age 3 or under; see "Button Rx" above.

INSTRUCTIONS

Cut the belting into two equal lengths.

Thread each end of each belting length through the top loop of a suspender clip; adjust the belting until the suspenders fit the child and trim

any excess, leaving approximately 3" at each suspender end for growth adjustment.

Using a narrow satin stitch, edge-finish the belting ends; securely hand tack the belting ends to the belting back at the position determined (Figure 2). *Note:* For a quicker, more permanent method, satin stitch through both layers at the belting raw ends; the stitching will show on the right side.

Using the photo on page 21 as a guide, arrange each set of buttons in a vertical row on the

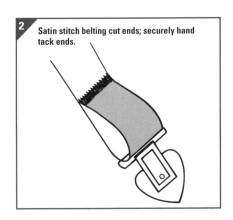

2 Satin stitch belting cut ends; securely hand tack ends.

suspender fronts and securely stitch them to the belting.

❏

— PIPING PLEASURE —

Whether you make your own or purchase this nifty notion for embellishing children's apparel and other projects, piping adds a decorative detail to define edges and seams and is often the perfect accent.

The following instructions detail how to achieve perfectly piped seams and edges. For instructional purposes, we refer to the item to which the piping will be applied as a garment, however, this same method can be used on other projects as well. To apply perfect piping:

Pin piping to the right side of one garment section, matching the piping stitching line to the garment seamline and matching raw edges.

For curves and corners, clip the piping seam allowances and ease in extra fullness to prevent these areas from pulling or cupping under (Figure 1).

Using a zipper or cording foot, machine baste the piping in place along the piping stitching line.

1 On curves and corners, clip piping seam allowances to prevent pulling and cupping.

Pin the garment sections right sides together and stitch the seam just to the *left* of the first row of stitching.

For enclosed seams, grade and clip the seam allowances; turn right side out and press.

❏

SEW, YOU'RE A MOM!

Enjoy that nine months of anticipation, planning, excitement—and sewing—to welcome your tiny new arrival. New mommies are faced with so many impending changes, and getting the nursery and all baby's necessities assembled and organized can bring some of that little cherub's joy just a little bit early. And when you see that delicate, innocent face peer into your eyes for the very first time, all your efforts will be put into perspective.

We shared with you the fundamentals of creating nursery requisites in "Babes In Nurseryland" (page 13), and you're covered in terms of bib basics ("Drool-Cool Bibs," page 16), hair accents for baby girls ("Banded Beauty," page 17) and tiny toys for learning tots ("Blocks For Babes," page 14). Now, we would like to offer you accessory projects—some simple, some serious—for welcoming baby into your life.

Use leftover fabric scraps from your nursery-decorating adventure to make the fabric-covered frames in "Baby Frame-Up" coordinate with your nursery's soft furnishings before baby's arrival. Or, wait until baby makes a grand entrance, then quickly assemble a frame in either pink or blue to complement that first photograph. Creativity and a bit of imagination will help you embellish these frames with such extras as lace or dainty juvenile buttons for three-dimensional interest.

The delicate stocking in "Baby's First Christmas" will inspire thoughts and planning of your most special Christmas yet—baby's first. Rendered in tiny gingham and decorated with appliqués, ribbons and lots of lace, this pint-sized pretty will also be right at home as a nursery door ornament after the holidays have come and gone. If your tastes lean more toward the traditional, don't hesitate to fabricate this little wonderment in Christmas reds, greens and golds for a totally different, but just as juvenile look.

"Baptismal Bliss" is an inspirational story on creating your child's christening gown, replete with illustrations on all kinds of laces and lace insertions for embellishment and how-tos for creating your own "heirloom yardage." And "Baby Cuddle-Up" lets you show off your creative serging skills on an oversized receiving blanket, rendered in soft flannel. This will be one of the easiest to sew and most often used projects you'll create.

Enjoy the months preceding the birth of your baby, letting these accessories set a loving, home-spun foundation for your new little darling. ❏

baby frame-up!

Your cherished cherub's photo deserves a place of honor in the nursery. For a decorator touch, coordinate the frame with the nursery furnishings by fabric-covering a frame using left-over remnants, then embellish to your heart's delight to create just the right look to complement your style—and your baby's!

MATERIALS

For up to an 11"x14" frame:

• Pre-cut cardboard matboard with backer board and easel in your choice of size and shape, or non-corrugated cardboard to cut your own frame pieces

• ½ yard of 45"-wide fabric

• ½ yard of 6- to 8-ounce polyester batting

• White craft glue

• Lace or other trim the length of the frame perimeter plus 1"

• 2½" to 3" of ⅜"-wide ribbon

• Clothespins or large paper clips

PREPARATION

■ Each fabric-covered frame will require the components shown in Figure 1. If you're cutting your own matboard, cut the backer board ⅛" smaller than the front board and score the easel ½" from the upper edge. *Note:* If you plan to hang the frame on the wall, eliminate the easel.

CONSTRUCTION

■ Position the front board on the fabric wrong side; trim the fabric to 1" larger than the front board on all outer edges.

■ Center the frame on the fabric wrong side and trace the photo opening. Remove the board and draw a second line ¼" inside the opening line. Cut out the opening along the inside line (Figure 2, page 147).

■ Glue the batting to one side of the front board and trim the batting even with the board edges. Set the front board aside until the glue dries.

■ To face the photo opening, center a matching fabric scrap 1½" larger than the opening over the front board fabric right sides together (Figure 3, page 147); stitch on the photo opening line. Trim the seam to ¼" and clip the curves; press the facing to the wrong side.

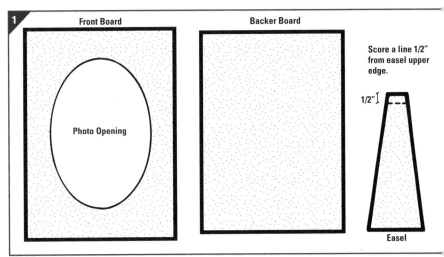

1

Front Board

Photo Opening

Backer Board

Score a line 1/2" from easel upper edge.

1/2"

Easel

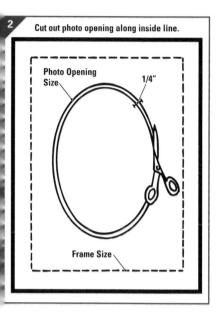

2 Cut out photo opening along inside line.

Photo Opening Size

1/4"

Frame Size

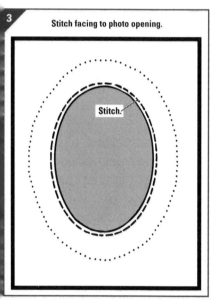

3 Stitch facing to photo opening.

Stitch.

■ Center the front board batting-side-down on the faced fabric wrong side. Stretch and wrap the facing through the front board photo opening to the wrong side; finger press

the seam allowances toward the facing.

Glue the facing edges to the front board wrong side, aligning the seamline with the photo opening edge (Figure 4); secure the glued edges with clothespins or clips until the glue dries. Trim the facing as needed to prevent it from extending beyond the frame outer edges.

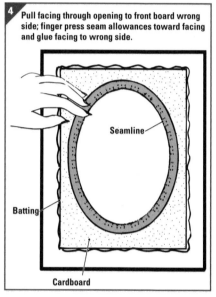

4 Pull facing through opening to front board wrong side; finger press seam allowances toward facing and glue facing to wrong side.

Seamline

Batting

Cardboard

■ To cover the backer board while the front board glue dries, place the backer board right side down on the fabric wrong side; trim the fabric to 1" larger than the board. Stretch and wrap the fabric to the backer board wrong side, gluing the edges to the board and holding them in place until the glue dries.

■ Cut a second piece of fabric ⅛" smaller than the backer board and glue it to the backer board wrong side, covering the raw edges from the previous step (Figure 5).

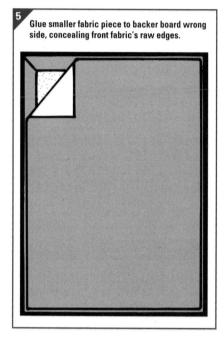

5 Glue smaller fabric piece to backer board wrong side, concealing front fabric's raw edges.

■ Cover the easel using the above backer board procedure.

■ To complete the front board (when the glue is completely dry), stretch and wrap the fabric outer edges tautly over the batting and glue them to the board wrong side outer edges; clip and/or "pleat" the fabric edges as needed to create a smoother surface. Anchor the fabric with clothespins or clips until the glue dries (Figure 6, page 148).

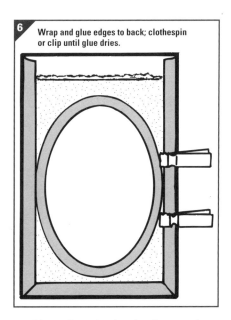

6 Wrap and glue edges to back; clothespin or clip until glue dries.

■ Glue the desired trim or lace right side finished edge to the front board wrong side outer edge, easing the trim around the corners and butting the ends inconspicuously (Figure 7).

7 Glue trim around frame edges, easing corners and butting ends.

FINISHING

■ Glue the front board to the backer board at the outer edges, leaving space for inserting the photo: On square or rectangular frames, glue only three edges; on oval or round frames, leave an opening slightly wider than your photo (Figure 8). Hold the edges in place until the glue dries.

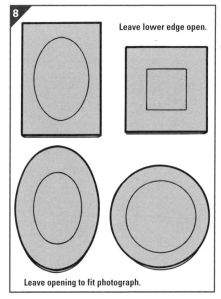

8 Leave lower edge open.

Leave opening to fit photograph.

■ Position the easel on the frame back so the frame sits evenly on a surface. Glue the area above the score line to the frame back. Glue one end of the ⅜"-wide ribbon near the easel lower edge, the other end approximately 1" from the frame lower edge (Figure 9).

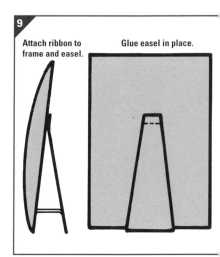

9 Attach ribbon to frame and easel. Glue easel in place.

■ Slide the photo into the frame. *Note:* On round or oval frames, it may be necessary to trim the photo before inserting it in the frame. ❑

This warm-weather T is a favorite to wear over fitted leggings—especially the printed variety—for today's kids. The drawstring waist is the detail of note, creating a fun peplum effect with an air of ease.

Render it in long or short sleeves in fabrics from lightweight interlock knits to heavier-weight sweatshirt fleeces in solid, striped and printed varieties.

While this concept is simple—a basic silhouette "cinched" at the waist with either elastic, drawstring or a combination of the two—ready-to-wear prices for the clever little number can be downright complex.

Kids will love this project! Let them choose the T-shirt and tie-dye it and a pair of leggings for a great look. Or opt for a bright solid T with striped or floral leggings. Whatever you and your child choose, don't make a big deal about shaping up your child's basic big T; let it retain its easy-going nature while taking on an updated look.

You or your child can duplicate this concept with minimal work, using an oversized T-shirt (sewn or purchased), ¼"-wide matching cording the length of the child's waistline measurement plus 1 yard, one package of matching extra-wide, double-fold bias tape, matching thread and a water-soluble marker.

■ Turn the T-shirt wrong side out and place it on a flat working surface.
■ Using a water-soluble marker, draw a line around the T-shirt 3" to 6" from the lower edge, depending on the child's size (Figure 1).

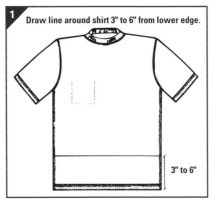

1 Draw line around shirt 3" to 6" from lower edge.

3" to 6"

■ Measure across the T-shirt from one side to the other and multiply this measurement by two; cut a piece of bias tape this length.
■ Unfold the bias tape once; press. Place the bias tape on the drawn line so the raw edges are concealed, beginning and ending at the shirt center front. Turn under each raw end ½", creating a 1" gap at the center, and pin the bias tape edges in place (Figure 2). Edgestitch the bias tape in place along both long edges.

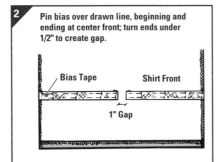

2 Pin bias over drawn line, beginning and ending at center front; turn ends under 1/2" to create gap.

Bias Tape   Shirt Front

1" Gap

■ Stitch two ½"-long vertical buttonholes ½" apart in the gap between the bias strip ends (Figure 3). *Note:* On lightweight knits, use a square of tear-away stabilizer behind the buttonholes to prevent stretching.

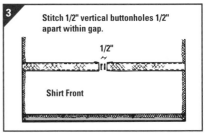

3 Stitch 1/2" vertical buttonholes 1/2" apart within gap.

1/2"

Shirt Front

■ Turn the T-shirt right side out. Using a bodkin or narrow safety pin and beginning on the shirt right side, thread the drawstring through one buttonhole, then through the bias casing and out the other buttonhole; knot each drawstring end (Figure 4).

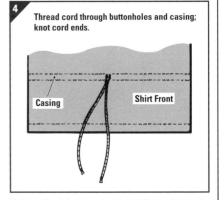

4 Thread cord through buttonholes and casing; knot cord ends.

Casing   Shirt Front

■ Try the T-shirt on the child, adjust the gathers and tie the cord ends into a bow; trim the cord if necessary and re-knot the ends. ❏

baby's first Christmas

This precious stocking is perfect for a newborn's first Christmas, its delicate pastel embellishments symbolic of the tiny innocent being for which it is intended. The stocking makes an extra-special shower gift, too, when filled with tiny findings for baby's nursery.

MATERIALS

- ¼ yard of light blue or pink quilted gingham
- ¼ yard of coordinating mini-dot fabric
- ½ yard of 2"-wide white gathered eyelet lace
- ½ yard of 1"-wide white gathered eyelet lace
- 1 yard of ⅛"-wide pink mini-dot satin ribbon
- ⅞ yard of 1¼"-wide white picot-edge ribbon
- ¾ yard of ⅝"-wide light blue-on-light blue striped sheer picot-edge ribbon
- ½ yard of ⅛"-wide white satin ribbon
- ½ yard of ⅛"-wide coordinating novelty print ribbon
- ½ yard each of two coordinating ¼"-wide novelty print ribbons
- Scraps of the following: ⅜"-wide coordinating novelty ribbon; ¼"-wide white flat lace trim; pink calico fabric; and white with pastel flowers fabric
- 10 small ribbon rosebuds (four hot pink, three white and three light blue)
- One ¾"-long white teddy bear button
- One pair of white diaper pins
- Fusible transfer web
- White craft glue
- Air-soluble marker
- Matching or contrasting thread
- Pattern tracing cloth

CONSTRUCTION

■ Apply fusible transfer web to the wrong side of the white with pastel flowers fabric and the calico fabric.

■ Enlarge the patterns in Figure 1, page 151. Cut two stockings each (one of each in reverse) from the gingham and the mini-dot fabric for the stocking body and lining, respectively. From the fused calico, cut one bassinet trim; from the remaining fused fabric, cut one bassinet.

■ Remove the fusible web backing paper from the bassinet and bassinet trim, then fuse the bassinet in place on one gingham stocking (front) right side, according to the stocking pattern's placement guidelines and following the manufacturer's instructions; repeat to fuse the bassinet trim to the bassinet.

■ Using matching or contrasting thread and a medium-width zigzag satin stitch, appliqué the bassinet and bassinet trim in place (see "Super Satin Stitching" on page 76 for tips on successful satin stitching).

■ Cut a 2"-long piece of flat lace trim and topstitch it in place along the bassinet front edge (Figure 2, page 151).

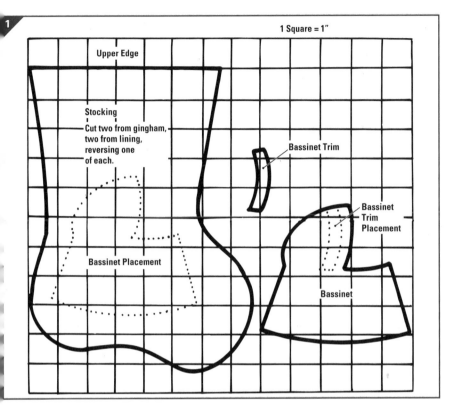

1 1 Square = 1"

Upper Edge

Stocking
Cut two from gingham,
two from lining,
reversing one
of each.

Bassinet Trim

Bassinet
Trim
Placement

Bassinet Placement

Bassinet

■ Cut a 5"-long piece of the ⅜"-wide novelty print ribbon, turn the raw ends under and edgestitch it in place along the bassinet upper edge, concealing the upper ruffle's gathered edge.

■ Make a six-loop bow from 12" of the ⅛"-wide white satin ribbon and tack it in place to the bassinet trim lower edge; glue a pink rosebud to the bow center (Figure 4).

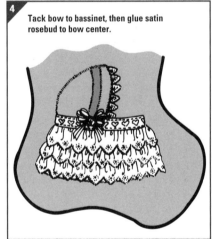

4 Tack bow to bassinet, then glue satin rosebud to bow center.

the lower row, overlapping each row slightly and turning under the ends of each, as shown in Figure 3.

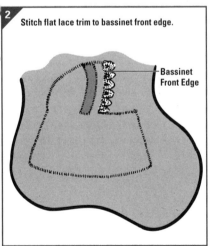

2 Stitch flat lace trim to bassinet front edge.

Bassinet Front Edge

3 Stitch gathered lace strips in place, beginning with lower edge row, overlapping each slightly and turning raw ends under.

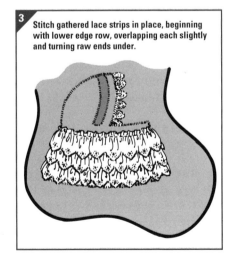

■ Cut three 5"-long pieces of 1"-wide gathered eyelet lace; stitch them in place on the bassinet body to create a ruffled skirt effect, beginning with

■ Right sides together, sew the gingham stockings together in a ¼" seam, leaving the upper edge open for turning. Clip the curves and turn the stocking right side out.

■ Stitch a row of the 2" gathered eyelet lace around the stocking 1" below the stocking upper edge, turning the lace ends under (Figure 5, page 152).

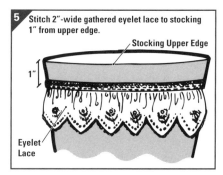

5 Stitch 2"-wide gathered eyelet lace to stocking 1" from upper edge.

Stocking Upper Edge

1"

Eyelet Lace

■ Stitch three rows of novelty print ribbon (two ¼"-wide, one ⅛"-wide) above the eyelet lace, concealing the lace upper edge, abutting the ribbon long edges and turning the ribbon ends under (Figure 6).

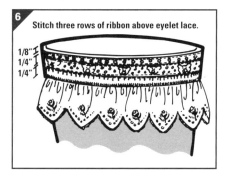

6 Stitch three rows of ribbon above eyelet lace.

1/8"
1/4"
1/4"

■ Right sides together, stitch the stocking linings together in a ⅜"-wide seam; trim the seam to a scant ⅛" and clip the curves. *Note:* Do *not* turn the stocking lining right side out.

■ *Wrong* sides together, place the stocking lining into the stocking body. Turn under the upper edge of each stocking ¼" and slipstitch the stocking to the lining along the upper edge (Figure 7).

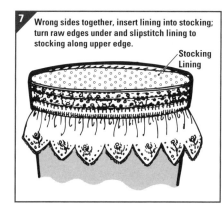

7 Wrong sides together, insert lining into stocking; turn raw edges under and slipstitch lining to stocking along upper edge.

Stocking Lining

■ Make three ribbon rosebud clusters, each with one hot pink, one white and one light blue rosebud, and glue each cluster in place at the bassinet lower edge; tack the teddy bear button to the bassinet upper edge (Figure 8).

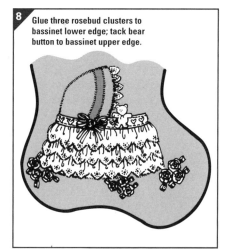

8 Glue three rosebud clusters to bassinet lower edge; tack bear button to bassinet upper edge.

■ Make a four-loop bow from both the white and light blue picot-edge ribbons. Right sides up, center and tack the blue bow to the white bow, then tie

the ⅛"-wide pink mini-dot ribbon around the center of the bows and tie it into a bow as well (Figure 9).

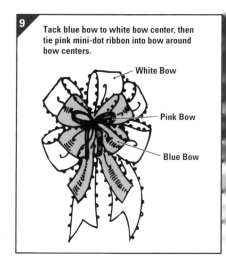

9 Tack blue bow to white bow center, then tie pink mini-dot ribbon into bow around bow centers.

White Bow

Pink Bow

Blue Bow

■ Secure the diaper pins to the bow centers with a double knot, then glue the bow/pin cluster to the stocking upper left edge.

■ Fold the remaining 6" of ⅛"-wide white satin ribbon in half to make a hanging loop; tack the loop in place to the stocking inside at the upper left edge. ❏

baptismal bliss

Steeped in tradition, the christening gown makes the ideal heirloom garment. Unlike wedding dresses which can vary greatly according to current fashion and the bride's style and size, christening gowns have changed very little throughout past decades—probably because babies and the purpose of these gowns have changed so little. And there's never a worry about fit—all babies begin as tiny beings.

Traditional christening gowns were made of fine cotton or linen—the only fabrics available a century ago—and embellished with laces, ruffles and decorative hand sewing, such as pintucking and hemstitching. Peruse any current pattern catalog, and you'll see the only modified element is the sewing method, specifically, sewing by machine as opposed to by hand. Even the serger is being utilized in some designs. The result: easier and speedier techniques for creating your own original heirloom—whether a design of your own device or one duplicated from an old family photo.

HEIRLOOM FINERY

The following tips will help you get started in your heirloom-sewing venture.

■ Use fine cotton batiste or broadcloth or a more economical blend of polyester and cotton, keeping in mind that while synthetic blends are less expensive and wrinkle-resistant, they may pucker between rows of pintucks and lace.

■ Choose the best quality fine cotton laces you can afford. And remember: Fewer rows of a quality cotton lace will be much prettier—and easier to handle—than many rows of an inexpensive, lower-quality synthetic trim.

■ Use extra-fine sewing thread and a new size 70/11 sewing machine needle.

■ Consider some of the following adornments, available in the trims section of your favorite fabric store:

• *Entredeux.* This trim, which features a strip of cut-out holes between two seam allowances, resembles hemstitching and may be applied between strips of fabric or laces as a decorative seam reinforcement (Figure 1).

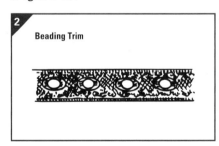

1
Entredeux Trim

• *Beading.* This trim features woven openings to accommodate narrow ribbon woven in and out of the openings (Figure 2).

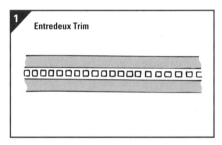

2
Beading Trim

• *Lace Insertion.* As its name implies, lace insertion is a lace trim with two straight edges that can be stitched (inserted) between fabric pieces or other trims (Figure 3, page 154).

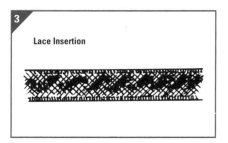

Lace Insertion

• *Lace Edging.* This trim features only one straight edge, which can be applied to a neck, sleeve or hem edge (Figure 4).

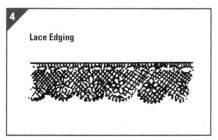

Lace Edging

• *Embroidered Insertion.* Featuring two raw edges and an embroidered design, this trim is applied like lace insertion (Figure 5).

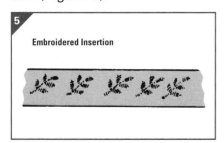

Embroidered Insertion

EMBELLISHED FABRIC STRIPS

Beautiful and inexpensive effects can be created without trims, too, by simply embellishing fabric strips with pintucking (see your machine manual for details and instructions) or puffing, a technique that involves gathering fabric strips along both long edges, then using these strips as insertions (Figure 6).

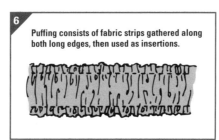

Puffing consists of fabric strips gathered along both long edges, then used as insertions.

Traditional pintucks are formed by stitching $\frac{1}{16}$" or $\frac{1}{8}$" from a folded edge, and because most all-cotton, fine fabrics finger-press so well, you won't even need to leave your sewing machine to stitch an entire series of pintucks. Some machines will allow you to move the needle position to help you form the desired pintuck width. *Note:* All pintucks should be stitched in the same direction to prevent distortion and "drag" lines, then pressed to one side.

Twin-needle pintucks require even less preparation than the single-needle variety. Consult your machine manual for specifics on using the twin needle and pintuck foot for the most efficient results.

DESIGN DETAILS

These guidelines will help you achieve the most desirable effects in a christening gown.

■ Begin with a simple christening gown pattern or simple dress pattern, adding length to a dress pattern as necessary (christening gowns are generally at least 34" long from the back neck to the hemline), and embellish! Add a fancy band or ruffle at the hem; edge the collar and sleeve hems with lace; add pintucks and insertions to the dress body or sleeves; and most of all, use your creativity for a one-of-a-kind design.

■ Consider creating "heirloom yardage," then cutting a pattern piece, such as a yoke or the sleeves, from that yardage (Figure 7). To do so:

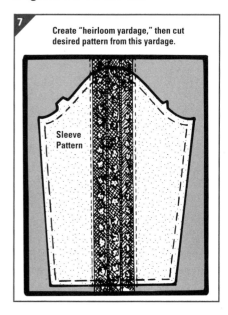

Create "heirloom yardage," then cut desired pattern from this yardage.

Sleeve Pattern

• Accumulate fabric or trim strips that are at least 2" longer than the widest or longest part of the garment piece to be embellished, depending on whether you'll be applying the trims vertically or horizontally on the garment section (Figure 8).

• Experiment with the trim placement by laying the trims over the fabric until you achieve a desirable design (Figure 9), envisioning incorporating pintucks as well, if desired. Take note of the trim placement and spacing before removing the trims from your test piece.

• If possible, apply all embellishments on the crosswise grain to lessen or prevent puckering.

• Lightly mark the trim placement lines on the fabric piece with a water-soluble marker, or pull a thread for placement lines that are perfectly on-grain.

• As you construct the design, begin in the center and add a piece of trim to one side, then the other, alternating back and forth to achieve the most symmetrical results.

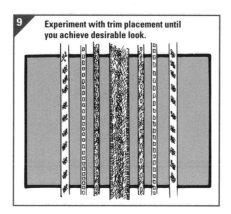

9 Experiment with trim placement until you achieve desirable look.

• Press the finished yardage, allow it to cool, then cut out the garment piece.

ASSEMBLY

■ Spray starch and press all fabric strips and trims, with the exception of puffing, before joining them together.

■ When applying lace to lace, simply butt the two strips together along straight one edge and zigzag to secure them in a near-invisible joining, setting the stitch just wide enough (2 to 3) to catch the trim headings and just long enough (1 to 1.5) to be nearly invisible (Figure 10) and beginning ¼" to ⅜" in from the ends to avoid machine jams.

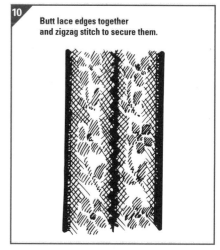

10 Butt lace edges together and zigzag stitch to secure them.

■ Use the above-described butting and zigzagging technique to apply lace edging to a folded edge, such as the hem edge of a sleeve or skirting.

■ To join flat lace to entredeux, trim off one entredeux seam allowance, then butt one lace edge against the trimmed entredeux edge; set the zigzag stitch length so one side of the zigzag swings into a hole of the entredeux, the other side swings just inside the lace (Figure 11, page 156).

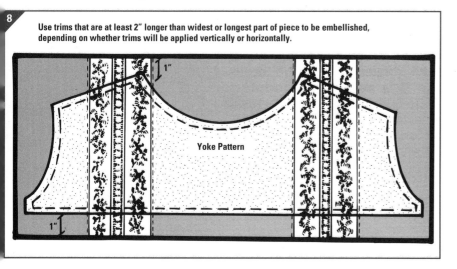

8 Use trims that are at least 2" longer than widest or longest part of piece to be embellished, depending on whether trims will be applied vertically or horizontally.

Yoke Pattern

1"

1"

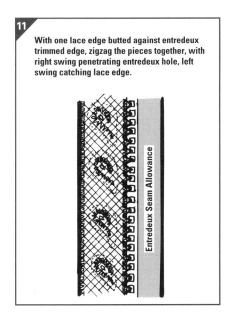

11 With one lace edge butted against entredeux trimmed edge, zigzag the pieces together, with right swing penetrating entredeux hole, left swing catching lace edge.

Entredeux Seam Allowance

■ Use the "rolling and whipping" technique to join laces and entredeux to fabric strips or embroidered insertion; the seam allowances are zigzagged so they actually roll or curl to create a neat and durable narrow seam. The two variations are as follows:

To apply entredeux to flat fabric:

• Right sides together, place the entredeux seam allowance along the fabric strip raw edge.

• Straight stitch along the entredeux right-hand side, as close to the holes as possible (Figure 12).

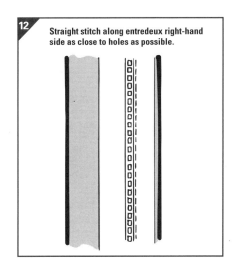

12 Straight stitch along entredeux right-hand side as close to holes as possible.

• Trim the fabric and entredeux seam allowance to a scant ⅛" (Figure 13).

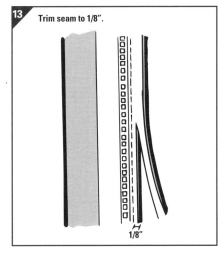

13 Trim seam to 1/8".

1/8"

• Using a zigzag stitch set so the left swing penetrates an entredeux hole and the right swing extends just beyond the seam allowance edge, zigzag along the entire length of entredeux, securing it to the fabric (Figure 14). The fabric will roll into the seam.

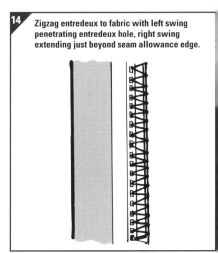

14 Zigzag entredeux to fabric with left swing penetrating entredeux hole, right swing extending just beyond seam allowance edge.

• Press the trim and fabric flat.

To apply flat lace, such as embroidered or lace insertions, beading or lace edging, to flat fabric:

• Right sides together, place the lace on top of the fabric, with the fabric edge extending ⅛" beyond the lace right-hand edge (Figure 15).

15 Place lace and fabric right sides together, with 1/8" of fabric edge extending.

1/8"

• Satin stitch the lace in place, with the left swing of the zigzag penetrating the lace edge, the right swing extending just beyond the fabric edge (Figure 16).

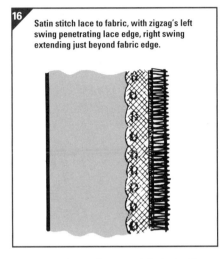

16 Satin stitch lace to fabric, with zigzag's left swing penetrating lace edge, right swing extending just beyond fabric edge.

• Press the trim and fabric flat.

• For additional durability, zigzag over the seam from the right side, setting the stitch width just wide enough (.5 to 1.5) to span the narrow rolled seam underneath and just long enough (1 to 2) to be almost invisible (Figure 17).

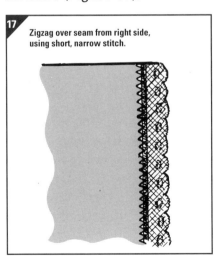

17 Zigzag over seam from right side, using short, narrow stitch.

FINISHING DETAILS

■ Examine the interior of any heirloom christening gown and you'll likely see the fine finish of French seams. The result of this three-step process is a narrow seam allowance on the garment inside that encases the raw edges (Figure 18). To duplicate this finish:

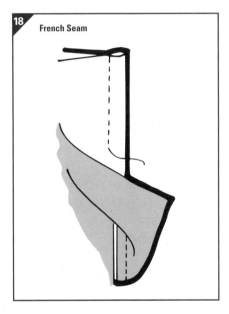

18 French Seam

• Raw edges matching, place the garment pieces *wrong* sides together; stitch in a ⅜" seam, using a short stitch length.

• Trim the seam allowances to ⅛" and press them to one side.

• Fold the garment *right* sides together along the seam, encasing the seam allowance between the fabric right sides; press.

• From the garment wrong side, stitch a seam ¼" from the fold and press the seam allowance to one side.

■ Today, serger users can opt for the speed of a serger rolled hem to achieve a similar narrow finish. This technique is especially handy for curved seams which are unsuitable for French seams. For durability, straight stitch the seam first on the conventional machine, then switch to the serger rolled edge and serge the length of the seam, trimming the excess seam allowance simultaneously. *Note:* Use texturized nylon thread for a very soft seam finish.

■ French binding is another finishing option. It's neat and attractive at the neckline in lightweight fabrics and eliminates the need for a facing. To do this:

• Trim away the neckline seam allowance, if applicable.

• Cut a 1¾"-wide bias fabric strip 1" longer than the neckline edge.

• Fold the strip in half lengthwise, wrong sides together, and press lightly.

• Use your iron to shape the bias strip to match the neckline curve.

• Right sides together and raw edges matching, pin the binding to the neckline; stitch in place in a ¼" seam. If desired, sandwich gathered lace edging between the neckline and bias strip before stitching the strip in place.

• Turn under the ends at the neckline back opening and fold the bias strip over the seam allowances; press, then slip-stitch the remaining strip edge in place (Figure 19).

• Use a thread loop and pearl button for the back opening closure.

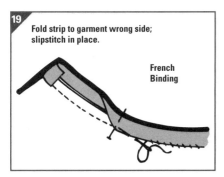

19

Fold strip to garment wrong side; slipstitch in place.

French Binding

❏

— SCALLOPED ELEGANCE —

Corded scallops add a delicate edging to almost any garment. Because they look like hand crocheted lace, these open scallops add an elegant touch to the collars, cuffs, tucks and hems of little girls' dresses, pinafores, jumpers, jumpsuits...

Corded scallops are sewn to a finished or folded edge. Since the scallops are actually stitched off the fabric edge, they must be sewn over cording, such as size 8 pearl cotton, and stitched on paper or tear-away stabilizer which is later removed. For the best results, the thread, cording and paper should be the same color.

■ Set the machine for a scalloped satin stitch (refer to your sewing machine manual for length, width and needle position settings), use an embroidery presser foot and tighten the bobbin tension.

■ Place the paper under the fabric so it extends 1" beyond the fabric edge.

■ Position the fabric edge so only the scallop *point* catches the fabric.

■ Hold the cord loosely in your right hand while guiding the fabric with your left hand (Figure 1).

■ When the stitching is complete, carefully tear the paper away.

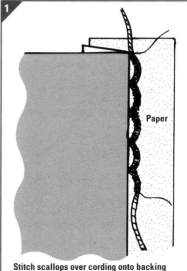

1

Paper

Stitch scallops over cording onto backing paper, then tear paper away.

❏

color photo of finished project on page 22

baby cuddle-up

Expectant mothers generally experience what the experts call "nesting" instincts, preparing baby's environment for the most loving and nurturing setting possible. And for expectant moms who are also fashion-sewers, the sewing machine and serger will likely play significant roles in building the "nest"—ideas abound for creating your own nursery accessories and infant layettes. Few projects are as easy to sew or as readily used and needed as the receiving blanket. When you put your serger to work with a variety of decorative threads and soft, cuddly blanketing, such as a breathable, washable cotton flannel, practical will be anything but boring—even if you make the requisite six to 12 blankets needed for new babies.

MATERIALS

• 1¼ yards of 45"-wide printed cotton flannel, plus ⅛ yard for test stitching

• 1¼ yards of a 45"-wide solid-colored cotton flannel to coordinate with the print, plus ⅛ yard for test stitching

• Matching variegated pearl cotton thread

• Coordinating solid-colored pearl cotton thread

• Matching all-purpose thread

• Water-soluble marker

• Seam sealant, such as Fray Check™

• Tapestry needle

• Serger

SERGER SET-UP

Note: Prewash the fabrics before beginning; cut a 45" square from each fabric and save the scraps for test stitching.

■ Place the variegated thread in the upper looper, all-pur-pose thread in the needle and lower looper.

■ Adjust the serger for 3-thread flatlocking.

Note: If your serger has a 2-thread flatlocking capability, use the variegated thread in the looper, all-purpose thread in the needle, then follow your serger manual to adjust the appropriate tensions and do 2-thread instead of 3-thread flatlocking.

■ Select the widest stitch width and the desired stitch length.

■ Loosen the needle and upper looper tensions and tighten the lower looper tension considerably.

■ Test your stitch on scraps of your project fabric until the needle thread forms a "V" on the fabric underside, the lower looper thread lies in a straight line on the edge and the upper looper thread meets the needle thread at the edge (Figure 1).

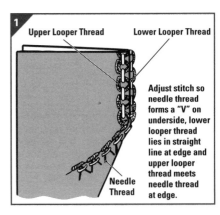

Upper Looper Thread   Lower Looper Thread

Adjust stitch so needle thread forms a "V" on underside, lower looper thread lies in straight line at edge and upper looper thread meets needle thread at edge.

Needle Thread

Note: If the upper looper tension is loosened completely

and the upper looper thread is still not loose enough to meet the needle thread at the edge (somewhat common when using heavy decorative threads), try removing the thread from one or more thread guides just above the tension dial. As a last resort, remove the thread from the tension dial (Figure 2).

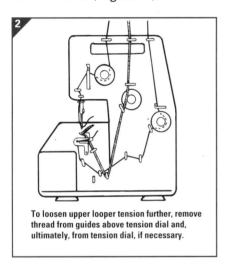

To loosen upper looper tension further, remove thread from guides above tension dial and, ultimately, from tension dial, if necessary.

CREATING "PATCHWORK"

Note: Stitch all rows in one direction first.

■ Fold the solid-colored flannel square in half and press.

■ Flatlock along the fold, serging *slowly* and guiding the fabric so the stitches protrude from the edge (Figure 3). Chain off at the end and clip the threads, leaving a short tail.

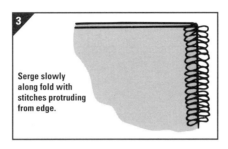

Serge slowly along fold with stitches protruding from edge.

■ Unfold the fabric, pulling the serging flat; press.

■ Working from the first row of flatlocking out toward the square raw edges, divide each half of the square into quarters, marking three flatlocking lines on each side of the flatlocking with the water-soluble marker (Figure 4).

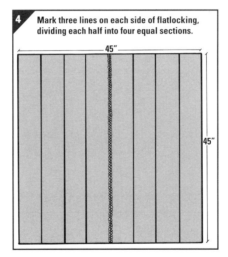

Mark three lines on each side of flatlocking, dividing each half into four equal sections.

45"

45"

■ Working on one marked line at a time: Fold the fabric along the marked line, press, then flatlock along the fold as instructed above for the first row of flatlocking; unfold the fabric, pulling the serging flat,

and press. Repeat along the remaining marked lines (Figure 5).

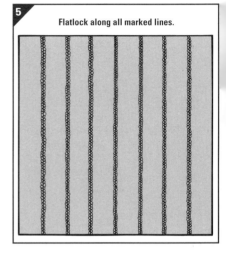

Flatlock along all marked lines.

■ Fold the flannel square in half in the opposite direction and flatlock seven evenly spaced rows in the same manner described above, forming a crisscross pattern; press flat (Figure 6).

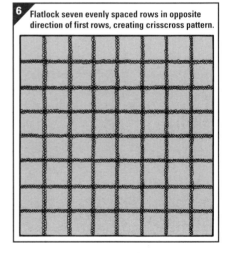

Flatlock seven evenly spaced rows in opposite direction of first rows, creating crisscross pattern.

RIBBON VARIATION

For added color interest, especially when you're unable to find a suitable variegated thread, flatlock over matching ⅛"- wide ribbon (the ribbon should be slightly narrower than the flatlock stitch). To do so:

■ Lengthen the stitch length to allow the ribbon to peek through the loops.

■ Fold and mark the fabric as instructed under "Creating Patchwork" above.

■ As you serge each row, guide the ribbon under the presser foot so it is encased in the stitch; the needle should *not* pierce the ribbon and the knife should *not* cut the ribbon (Figure 7). *Note:* If your serger has a tape/ribbon sewing guide, this accessory will keep the ribbon in place as you serge; see your serger manual for details.

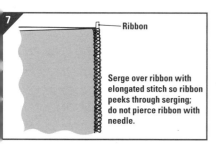

Serge over ribbon with elongated stitch so ribbon peeks through serging; do not pierce ribbon with needle.

■ Unfold the fabric and pull the stitching flat as instructed above (Figure 8), then proceed to serge each row.

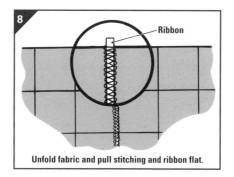

Unfold fabric and pull stitching and ribbon flat.

CONSTRUCTION

■ On a large, flat surface, place the printed and flat-locked squares *wrong* sides together, with raw edges matching; pin.

■ Using your conventional sewing machine, straight stitch the squares together; trim the edges even with each other, if necessary.

■ Set your serger for a balanced 3-thread stitch, using all-purpose thread in the needle, variegated pearl cotton in the upper looper and solid-colored pearl cotton in the lower looper.

■ Test your stitch on scraps of your project fabric (two layers). *Note:* Using heavy decorative thread in both loopers will generally require considerable tightening of the needle thread tension, loosening of the upper looper tension and a near-normal tension adjustment for the lower looper.

■ With the flatlocked square up, serge one raw edge of the flannel squares, serging off the edge at the corner; clip the threads, leaving a 3" tail.

■ Pivot the square and serge slowly to begin finishing the next raw edge; proceed in the same manner until all four raw edges are finished.

■ Neaten each corner by threading the tail through a tapestry needle and weaving it under 1" of serging; clip the thread ends (Figure 9). Secure the ends permanently with a *tiny* drop of seam sealant.

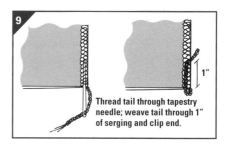

Thread tail through tapestry needle; weave tail through 1" of serging and clip end.

❏

SEWING FOR GROWING KIDS

Planning a wardrobe for growing children can be a real challenge, fraught with sudden growth spurts and stubborn likes and dislikes. If you've settled for ready-made clothing and accessory pieces that didn't meet your standards of quality just long enough and you would like to extend the normal lifetime of your child's wardrobe and other necessities, think ahead—then take a trip to the fabric store.

Sewing for kids can be as fulfilling and enjoyable as sewing for yourself—in fact, more so in many respects when you consider the project size and the involvement of your child. This will be a time for a meeting of the minds between you and your child as you dream and scheme together of things to sew to meet the child's needs—for either fun or function.

Sewing children's clothing has two major benefits (not unlike those associated with sewing for adults): Clothes can be tailor-made to fit any size child, and clothes can be personalized to reflect the child's style and personality.

PLANNING

Whether you're starting from scratch or adding a few garments to an existing wardrobe, give careful thought to fabric selection (see "Fabric" below). Comfort is key to children—their favorite garments are often the oldest, most bedraggled outfits in the closet. But they're comfortable and make the child feel good.

Give your child some choice in fabric selection, but keep in mind wearability and care and direct her or him accordingly. Knits are an excellent choice; their stretchability inherently provides growing room; they're fashionable and easy to sew. Bright colors are favorites, and they're easily seen by busy moms, motorists, and teachers as an added perk. Be aware, however, that the deep, dark colors can have a tendency to appear faded after just a few washings, and they need to be washed separately. Firmly woven fabrics, such as denim, poplin, twill and corduroy are durable for everyday wear. And more delicate fabrics and laces, although not as practical for playwear and school clothes, are certainly appropriate for special-occasion attire.

Choose a basic color scheme to provide some wardrobe flexibility. For example, sewing two to three tops to coordinate with one skirt or pair of pants can make getting dressed in the morning much easier for the budding fashion plate.

STYLING

When choosing designs for kids, measure accurately and follow the charts in the commercial pattern company catalogs to guide you in size selection (see "Sizing" below). Avoid the temptation to make a garment one or more sizes too large for longevity purposes. While a garment to "grow into" may seem like a rational idea to an adult, it's not wise or appealing from a child's viewpoint. Consider the fragile ego of the child taunted for wearing a too-large garment or one that looks like a hand-me-down.

Two-piece dressing is the wisest move for children during growth years. A shirt or blouse may fit long after the matching pants or skirt have become shockingly short.

As you and your child study the pattern choices, think carefully about design options and how growth can be built into these designs. Consider how the styling can be adapted for reinforcing stress points—armholes, buttonholes, crotch seams, knees and elbows—to add longevity.

SIZING

Children come in all shapes and sizes, and although pattern sizes are *related* to the child's age, many variations in a child's development and build will affect the actual size. Therefore, the correct pattern size for children is determined by the body measurements, not the child's age. Also, keep in mind there is little correlation between pattern sizes and ready-to-wear sizes, so don't base size considerations on ready-made clothing.

SIZE RANGES

As children grow, their proportions and the function of their clothing changes. To allow for this, pattern companies have established various size ranges for children with similar proportions and clothing needs. Look for this information in the back of each commercial pattern catalog.

Infants' patterns range in size from newborn to 18 months, and allowances are made for the ever-present diaper, frequent diaper changes, rapid growth and a disproportionately large head. Generally, infant designs are worn during the first year when babies typically triple their weight and increase their length by one-third.

Toddlers' patterns range in size from 1 to 4 and fit the child who has learned to walk until he or she is approximately 3 years old. These patterns accommodate the child's head, which remains large in proportion to its body, and the child's rapidly developing legs. Toddler dresses are shorter than children's sizes, and pants patterns include a diaper allowance.

Children's patterns, in sizes 2 to 6X, are drafted with the same chest and waist measurements as Toddlers' patterns, but they are proportioned for taller children with broader backs and shoulders. Because these patterns do not include a diaper allowance, they are smaller through the waist and hips.

Girls' and Boys' patterns range in size from 7 to 14 and 7 to 12, respectively, and accommodate longer, slimmer limbs and torsos.

MEASURING UP

Children's patterns include wearing ease, but do not have as much design ease as adult patterns. Therefore, the child's body measurements can be used with confidence to determine the correct pattern size.

Kids grow fast, so measure the child every time you begin a new garment. You'll need only one or two measurements to select the correct pattern size. However, you'll need several more to decide if and where the pattern needs adjusting.

To take your child's measurements:

■ Hold the tape measure snugly but not tightly.

■ Measure the child over his or her under garments.

■ Measure around the chest, waist and hips.

■ Measure the length of the arms, back waist and front waist.

■ Measure the crotch depth.

■ Measure the desired finished length of a skirt, dress and pants.

■ Measure the child's height.

For dresses, shirts or jackets, use the chest measurement to select the pattern size; for pants and skirts, use the waist measurement. When the measurements fall between two sizes, purchase the larger size and use a deeper seam allowance to stitch the side seams.

Before cutting out the pattern, compare the child's body measurements to the actual pattern measurements, keeping in mind most adjustments will be made in the length, not the width (see "Alterations" below).

FABRIC

Fabric is an important consideration when sewing children's clothing. Use the choice and preparation guidelines below to help you make the best and most practical decisions about fabric.

CHOICES

Choose high-quality fabrics so the garments will wash and wear well. A bargain isn't a bargain if it doesn't hold its shape and color after a few washings, and your time is much too valuable to spend sewing something that isn't going to look nice and afford wearability.

Fabrics for babies, toddlers and older children must be washable, durable, affordable and most of all comfortable. You can't beat 100-percent cotton for all these qualities.

Predominately cotton blends also work well, but polyester alone can be abrasive and scratchy to delicate young skin. Also, 100-percent polyester is not breathable like natural fibers and is therefore hotter to wear in the warmer months, cooler in the cold months.

Good fabric choices include cotton varieties of broadcloth, poplin, denim, lightweight corduroy, velveteen and batiste and some washable wools.

When choosing fabric, also consider the fabric weight and scale of the print, and keep the fabric appropriate for small children. Contrary to the opinions of some people, kids can be quite helpful when choosing fabrics, so take them along to the fabric store if they're old enough to offer their opinions.

PREPARATION

Preshrink all fabrics and trims for kidswear—children grow fast enough without adding to the problem with shrinkage! Treat the fabric and notions as you will the finished garment, usually with at least one trip through the washing machine and dryer. Prewash denim three times to eliminate residual shrinkage.

Save fabric scraps from all projects—you might need them at the first growth spurt.

ALTERATIONS

Careful pattern choices and the addition of a few designer growth features makes good sense for all developing children, regardless of their age. They'll love the updated looks you can give their clothes, and you'll love the potential money savings.

LENGTH ADJUSTMENTS

Children tend to grow taller much faster than they grow wider, so think creatively as garments become too short. The easiest length adjustments are made at an already existing edge, such as a hemline or cuff, so build in growth before constructing the garment. Then follow these tips for "extending" the length of your child's garments.

■ Let out a dress or skirt hem, pulling it out carefully to leave the least possible trace of the original hem. If necessary, remove the original hem mark by spraying the fold with white vinegar, rubbing gently, then washing the garment. To re-hem:

• Fold the new hem so the stitching line exactly follows the former hem lower edge. The slight difference in coloration at the new hemline will be camouflaged by the hemming process.

• Or, add multiple rows of narrow tucks parallel to the hemline, camouflaging the original hemline and adding interest to the new hemline.

■ Add a coordinating appliquéd border to a skirt or dress hem. Then, coordinate the blouse cuffs and collar to the border edging. This serves a dual function of lengthening the sleeves as well.

Keep in mind borders don't *have* to be placed at a garment lower edge; consider using a border as an inset a few inches from the garment lower edge instead. Be sure, however, to sew inset borders in place evenly or the look will appear blatantly homemade.

Also, remember that fabric is crucial to the success of lengthening a garment with a border—the fabric must be the same weight and texture and have the same care requirements as the original garment.

Because wear changes the original garment colors, contrasting border fabrics are recommended. Consider, for example, jade green with navy blue or black with white. Another fabric suggestion is the use of plaid (or another print) borders with solid skirts or dresses.

■ Add a hip yoke to a too-short skirt, using matching fabric or a contrasting print for pattern-mixing or color-blocking appeal. If you choose a contrasting fabric, consider purchasing enough fabric to make a blouse as well to give the outfit an entirely new look.

■ Use ribbing for adding length to pant legs, sleeves and tummy-revealing T-shirts, adding a coordinating band or two to elongate the garment. For variety, add a ribbed neck band or collar to pull the look together.

■ Consider layering to gain a few more month's wear from a dress. For example, convert it into a tunic to wear over pants or a jumper to wear over tights or leggings.

■ Cut the suspenders of jumpers or overalls extra long for growth potential, simply moving the buttons with each growth spurt.

■ Use roll-up pant cuffs to provide many inches of growth for lanky legs. For safety, tack the rolled-up cuff at each side seam.

■ As a last resort for longer wear, consider changing the garment drastically. For example, make long pants into shorts, long sleeves into short sleeves on blouses and dresses, jumpsuits into shorts rompers.

WIDTH GROWTH ADJUSTMENTS

Although not as readily, children grow in girth, too, and some adjustments can be made in this area.

■ Add contrasting bands down the front of dresses and jumpers, down the side seams of shorts and pants. Also, use these stripes on matching T-shirts, adding them down the shoulder line—from the neck edge to the sleeve lower edge, and down the side seams—

from the underarm seam to the hemline edge.

■ Expand waistbands by converting them to an adjustable casing or by adding a decorative, elasticized band at the waistline.

■ When sewing for your child, keep in mind that design features like shoulder tucks, pleats, gathers and elasticized shirring build width wearing ease into a garment without extra planning. Also, garments with raglan sleeves and low-cut armholes don't bind with growth.

Whether you're a beginning fashion-sewer using simple-to-sew patterns or an advanced seamstress making heirloom garments, you'll achieve a feeling of pride and satisfaction watching your little ones parade around in garments you've sewn. Do yourself a favor and make time to sew. Each little custom-made creation is a memory in the making. ❏

— SEW ORGANIZED! —

Before you begin sewing a project for your child, read all the instructions—then use them as a *guide!* Most instructions are written in the easiest-to-understand-for-novice-sewers lingo, and experienced home-sewers can consider rearranging the suggested steps to save time.

Stretch your imagination to see how many sections of your project or garment you can sew consecutive-ly—assem-bly-line style—with-out stop-ping or cutting apart the pieces.

When sewing a favorite T-shirt for your youngster, for example, consider this process:

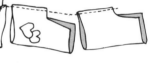

■ Stitch (or serge) the front and back together along one side seam, across one shoulder, across the second shoulder, then down the remaining side seam. Between sections, simply pull a bit of extra thread (or thread chain) as necessary.

■ Continue by sewing each sleeve underarm seam, joining the ribbing seams in the neckband, waistband and each sleeve band.

■ At this point, your sewn "train" might be reaching the floor behind your sewing machine, so stop to clip the pieces apart.

■ Complete the shirt by inserting the sleeves and attaching the ribbing bands.

The time you save with this continuous-sewing process can be used to spend with your little one, or go fabric shopping, or plan your next project... ❏

TENDER STITCHES

A youngster's flawless skin and smooth little body are more than just beautiful—they're *sensitive!*

Remember the fairy tale princess whose sleep was disturbed by one tiny pea hidden under layers of featherbeds? When you sew for a child, be prepared for a similar, real-life response.

Children balk at wearing clothing that itches, scratches or restricts their freedom of movement.

It's easy for today's busy home-sewer to become impatient when confronted by a picky "consumer." And you must admit, it hurts when an outfit you've made with such love languishes in the bottom of a drawer.

To avoid sewing a "reject," you must first define the challenges at hand. Obviously, each child's tolerance of discomfort is different. Some have more sensitive skin than others, for example. And some like clothes that hug the body, while others prefer loose, billowing styles.

Once you've assessed the limits of a particular child's comfort zone, you'll be most successful if you can "feel" the proposed garment from his or her point of view.

So take a deep breath and close your eyes for a moment. Think back to those days when *you* were the one unwillingly encased in that stiff, scratchy concoction known as the "party dress." Or maybe your friends decided to stage a somersault race on the day your mom made you wear those tourniquet-waisted shorts.

If it's all coming back to you, great! Now you're ready to throw your heart into creating outfits that the little princess (or prince) in your life will wear—and wear out—with pleasure.

Following are some of the most common hazards—and tips on how to avoid them.

APPLIQUÉ/EMBROIDERY ITCH

You've created the perfect appliqué or machine embroidered design, coordinating the colors and satin stitching without a waver. The final result is too cute for words. Then you hear the wail, "It itches! I can't wear it!"

If this scenario sounds all too familiar, or you fear such a scene with each loving stitch, consider the following tips:

■ Use lightweight machine embroidery thread in the bobbin and a close zigzag stitch *instead* of a true satin stitch. This will reduce thread bulk on the garment inside.

■ Appliqué or embroider garment portions that won't be worn next to the skin. For example, go wild on jackets and vests, or embellish pockets, collars, lined yokes, ruffles' outer tiers and knee patches.

■ Instead of stitching your appliqués to the garment, use fusible transfer web to secure them in place. Then finish the appliqué raw edges with fabric paint from a tube.

■ If you use a fabric stabilizer on the garment inside, be sure to remove as much of it as possible when you're finished embroidering or appliquéing. Then wash the garment to remove any excess stabilizer before the child tries it on.

■ Substitute iron-on designs for appliqués.

ELASTIC CONSTRICTION

If you're sewing for a child who is chubby or prefers loose clothing, patterns without defined waistlines are the obvious choice. Some examples include pinafores, high-waisted jumpsuits or jumpers and loosely constructed overalls.

But what if you plan to make a skirt, a dress with a waistline or a pair of pants? The following tips will help you make a garment that fits without constricting:

■ Use soft elastic, such as pajama elastic.

■ If the pattern design features a lot of fullness at the waistline, consider altering it to reduce the amount of gathering. Some children prefer fairly "flat" waistlines, and the extra gathers would only add pounds to an already chubby child.

■ Rely on the casing method of applying elastic until you know from experience how snug to make the waist. Also, leave excess elastic within the casing, and don't stitch the casing opening closed until the child has tried on the garment. This will allow for quick and easy adjustments.

■ Use fine lingerie elastic on sleeves, and remember that "loose is lovely" to a child's upper arms and wrists.

Some children hate *any* elastic on their arms. For these kids, substitute a pre-measured band with a button closure or a ribbing cuff (see "Cuff Lump Complaint" below). Another alternative is to just hem the sleeve edge if this suits the garment style.

■ Choose dress and jumpsuit patterns that feature a 2½"- to 4"-wide ribbing band to define the waistline. Other patterns can be converted to this style, too. *Note:* Remember to adjust the bodice and skirt or pant lengths if you use this technique.

TURTLENECK TORTURE

"I can't breathe! The neck is too high (too tight, pinches, is strangling me)!"

This is an easy problem to avoid, using one of several basic solutions:

■ Shorten the turtleneck height or create a similar look with a mock turtleneck.

■ Substitute a cowl collar, a ribbed band collar, a V-neck, a ruffled neckline edge, a standard rolled collar or whatever collar style the child prefers.

■ Enlarge the collar to fit the child's neck measurements or size preference for ease. Then compare the collar pattern size with one on an outfit the child likes and wears, if possible. Alter the collar and neck opening based on this measurement, if necessary.

CUFF LUMP COMPLAINT

If your young fashion model has this problem, you've got yourself a genuine, dyed-in-the-natural-cotton princess or prince. "Cuff Lump Complainers" prefer only the smoothest of surfaces to touch their sensitive wrists.

You can quell this complaint, however, if you're willing to take a little extra time. The following sewing "long-cuts" will help you construct comfortable cuffs:

■ Measure the cuff on a garment the child likes and wears, then compare this measurement to your pattern's finished cuff measurement. If necessary, adjust the pattern to allow more ease, keeping in mind no cuff, regardless of how smoothly it's constructed, will feel good if (in the child's opinion) it's too tight.

■ Substitute ribbing for cuffs designed to button. Many children prefer this softer, stretchier alternative, and you can use ribbed cuffs on sleeves made of woven as well as knit fabrics.

■ Apply ribbed cuffs to sleeves the "old-fashioned" way:

• Sew the underarm seam.

• Right sides together, sew the cuff ends together to form a circle.

• Right sides together, sew the cuff raw edges to the sleeve lower raw edge.

Although this method is more time-consuming and difficult than the shortcut method (sewing a flat cuff to a flat sleeve, then stitching the underarm and cuff seams simultaneously), the end result is a smooth inside finish on the cuff, similar to that of top-quality ready-wear apparel. Note: Many children prefer this construction method for ribbed necklines, too.

SERGED SEAM SENSITIVITY

You love your new serger and can't wait to save time and money duplicating those gorgeous ensembles seen in ready-to-wear. Before you go into mass production for little Jenny or Johnny, though, make a test garment for your little one's approval.

Some children find serged seams scratchy, compared to those you've zigzagged or simply double-stitched and trimmed. With the maddening inconsistency of youth, your child might even object to seams made on *your* serger, while breezily ignoring the same "problem" in ready-to-wear clothing.

Let's take a look at some ways you can derail the opposition and serge away with confidence:

■ Wash the garment before allowing the child to try it on. This will soften the seams enough that most youngsters will find them comfortable.

■ Construct ribbed necklines and cuffs using the "old-fashioned" method described under "Cuff Lump Complaint" above.

■ Topstitch serged seams flat to blend the seam allowance into the fabric. This works especially well with sweatshirting, since the fluffy fibers camouflage the seam after washing. To achieve the straightest topstitching possible, use a cording foot: Stitching from the garment right side, place the cording foot tunnel over the seam allowance, then offset the needle and sew away!

■ Increase your stitch length slightly, and experiment with stitch width to achieve seams that are strong enough for children's wear, yet don't have an uncomfortable thread buildup.

■ Use texturized nylon thread in your loopers. This will create a soft seam, such as those often found in ready-made pajamas, activewear and swimwear.

FABRIC PAINT PERSECUTION

It looks like such fun—and it is! In fact, your child can do it with you. Fabric painting is a great way to play Picasso or rival Renoir.

But remember: The inside of a painted garment can feel stiff. It can scratch. It can itch. Then you can guess who might not want to wear it!

The good news is you can fabric paint without these problems. To do so:

■ Avoid thick applications of "paint writers" from a tube on very lightweight fabrics, instead painting on fabrics with a bit of substance. A mediumweight interlock or woven fabric is fine, and sweatshirting is even better.

Using the proper fabric weight will minimize the stiffness caused by thick paint and will be less obvious when the garment is worn.

■ Apply paint with a brush sparingly, especially on lightweight fabrics. Some paints can be thinned before use, and new paint varieties make softer, more flexible designs.

■ If you want to go a little wild and use lots of thick paint regardless of your fabric weight, consider following the suggestions regarding embel-

lishment placement, as described in "Appliqué/ Embroidery Itch" above.

LACE LAMENT

Some little girls love to wear outfits festooned with lace that touches their skin. If you're sewing for one of the few, feel free to skip this section.

Aha, still reading! That's not surprising, since "Lace Lament" is one of the most common and plaintive tunes you're likely to hear if you create a frothy confection for that little lady.

Be assured, though, you can embellish an outfit with enough lace to make Scarlett O'Hara jealous, without leaving a telltale itch:

■ Decorate with abandon ruffles, pockets, roll-down collars, the buttonhole edge of garment fronts—any surface that doesn't touch the skin.

■ Apply lace on the outer surface of woven cuffs and stand-up collars, positioning the lace so it's flush with or slightly recessed from the finished edge.

■ Sandwich lace between the right side of ribbed collars or cuffs and the garment right side. Then stitch through all three layers, making sure the lace raw edge is fully encased within the seam allowances, so it can't irritate the skin.

■ Select soft lace for hemlines or sleeve finished edges.

■ If you can't resist adorning a jewel neckline with lace, position the lace so the ruffled edge extends down over the bodice. Since facings can cause the lace to flip up and tickle the child, try substituting a French seam or bias tape finish when covering the neckline seam allowances.

There's no question that making clothes for children is sewing at its best—a one-of-a-kind labor of love. And when you're alert to the particular sensitivities of the children in your sewing life, your finished products will be as comfortable as they are durable and beautiful. ❏

GATHER EASY!

The easiest way to gather a long strip of fabric or a bulky fabric is to place a heavy cord (buttonhole twist, crochet cord, pearl cotton or even dental floss!) just inside the seamline and zigzag over it with a long, wide stitch. Be careful *not* to catch the cord in the stitching, however, or this method won't work!

Knot one cord end to secure it, then pull on the other cord end to gather the fabric. Adjust the gathers evenly, then secure the other end of the cord. ❏

— TWO-FOR-ONE TOPSTITCHING —

Twin-needle topstitching produces two parallel rows of stitching at one time—a great look for hems on children's garments and other projects because it's secure, yet creates a subtle decorative effect (Figure 1).

Also, use the twin needle to topstitch facings and elastic and to attach pockets. To get started, all you need is a zigzag sewing machine and a twin needle (available at your local fabric store or sewing machine dealer).

Twin needles are available in sizes ranging from 1.6mm/size 70 to 4mm/size 100. The first number is the distance between the needles; the second is the

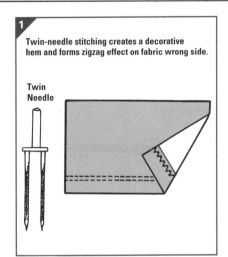

1

Twin-needle stitching creates a decorative hem and forms zigzag effect on fabric wrong side.

Twin Needle

size of the needles. A 2mm/size 80 is a good general-purpose twin needle.

To create twin-needle stitching:
- Using two spools of thread, follow the normal threading path with both threads. At the tension disc, place one thread on the left side of the disc, the other thread on the right side. At the last thread guide (just above the needle), place one thread in the left guide, the other in the right guide. If your machine has only one guide, place one thread in the guide and leave the other thread out.
- Set your machine for straight stitching; turn your machine's hand wheel to lower the needle slowly, checking that it doesn't hit the throat plate or presser foot.
- If skipped stitches occur, move the needle position slightly to the left.
- For stitching with a raised effect, tighten both the upper and lower thread tensions.

Twin-needle stitching—it's a two-for-one deal you'll be "sew" glad to discover! ❏

— BUTTONHOLE SAFETY —

To cut open buttonholes without worrying about cutting through the ends and ruining the project (children's or otherwise), follow this simple technique:
- Complete the buttonhole stitching, tie off all threads and dot each knot with a tiny bit of seam sealant.

Place a straight pin across each bartack end.

- Using your seam ripper or small scissors, pierce the buttonhole center and cut toward each end. The straight pin will act as a barrier, preventing you from cutting through the end of your stitching.

This method yields perfect buttonholes every time, without fear of slicing a project beyond repair with a careless slip of the "knife." ❏

CREDITS

 "terror-ific"

Drum Major created from premium-weight **Fruit of the Loom**® sweatshirt and sweatpants, available in children's sizes 2/4 to 14/16 at your local discount stores.

 "halloween in a hurry"

Bunny created from premium-weight **Fruit of the Loom**® sweatshirt and sweatpants, available in children's sizes 2/4 to 14/16 at your local discount stores.

11 **"bewitching capers"**

Witch's cape and hat fabricated in 50-percent cotton/50-percent polyester "Sew Scary" (print) and "Courtesy" (solid) from **Wamsutta OTC**, Dept. SN, 104 W. 40th St., New York, NY 10018.

12 **"hand-printed keepsake"**

Quilt fabricated in 100-percent cotton "When I Grow Up" from **VIP Fabrics**, Dept. SN, 1412 Broadway, New York, NY 10018.

14 **"blocks for babes"**

Soft blocks created with Scribbles® fabric paints from **Duncan Crafts** and ribbons and ribbon rosebuds from **C.M. Offray & Son Inc.**, both available at your local fabric and craft stores.

 "cowboy kudos"

Chaps and vest fabricated in "Camel" Ultrasuede® from **Ultrasuede Brand Fabrics**, Dept. SN, 104 W. 40th St., New York, NY 10018.

18 **"sew gifted"**

Nugget Belt and Windshield Scraper Mitt fabricated in Ultrasuede® ("Perry Pink" and "Camel," respectively) from **Ultrasuede Brand Fabrics**, Dept. SN, 104 W. 40th St., New York, NY 10018.
Towel Caddy and Cosmetic Bag fabricated in 100-percent cotton "Arabesque" from **Fabric-Traditions**, Dept. SN, 1350 Broadway, New York, NY 10018.

20 **"bow-dacious"**

Two-piece ensemble fabricated in 76-percent cotton/24-percent polyester "Lucern Velour" from **Dan River Inc.**, Dept. SN, 111 W. 40th St., New York, NY 10018. Bow appliqués fabricated in 100-percent acetate "King Purple," "Nu Ice" and "Nu Emerald" Bridal Satin from **Pago Fabrics**, Dept. SN, 48 W. 39th St., New York, NY 10018.

CREDITS cont...

21 "workout wow!"

Leotard fabricated in 85-percent nylon/15-percent Lycra® "Boutique Collection" coordinates from **Sew Easy Fabrics USA Ltd.**, Dept. SN, 107 New York Ave., Jersey City, NJ 07307.

21 "cute as a button"

"Multi-Motif Sneakers" and "Sprightly Suspenders" created with buttons and suspender clips from **JHB International Inc.**, available at your local fabric store.

22 "baby frame-up!"

Pastel-colored frames created with 50-percent cotton/50-percent polyester "Cozy Cafe—Playtime Pals" from **Springmaid**, Dept. SN, 104 W. 40th St., New York, NY 10018.

Primary-colored frame created with 50-percent cotton/50-percent polyester "Crayola Kids' Favorite Colors" from **Wamsutta OTC**, Dept. SN, 104 W. 40th St., New York, NY 10018. "Crayola Kids" and its logo are registered trademarks of **Binney & Smith**.

22 "baby's first Christmas"

Stocking created with ribbons and ribbon rosebuds from **C.M. Offray & Son Inc.**, and a bear button from **JHB International Inc.**, both available at your local fabric store.

NOTES

- -